FOR THE LOVE OF MIKE

FOR THE LOVE OF MIKE.

by Jo Wasson Hoyt

with Frank Graham, Jr.

NEW YORK ★ RANDOM HOUSE

First Printing

© *Copyright, 1966, by Jo Wasson Hoyt*
All rights reserved under International and Pan American Copyright
Conventions. Published in New York by Random House, Inc., and
simultaneously in Toronto, Canada, by Random House of Canada Limited.
Library of Congress Catalog Card Number: 66–21467
Manufactured in the United States of America
by H. Wolff, New York

To Charlotte and Branson for their patience and strength

Contents ★

FOR THE LOVE OF MIKE

1.

Rebellion

It was, ironically, on the comfortably familiar grounds of the American Consulate in Stanleyville that the mounting anxiety suddenly spilled over into violence. For days we had lived with that anxiety. Conflicting yet consistently frightening reports reached us from the revolt-torn provinces to the south. Rebel troops, some armed with Chinese Communist weapons, were advancing on this, the third largest city in the Congo. Carrying wands they believed would protect them from enemy bullets, the confident rebels advanced against scattered and dispirited government forces, who left behind their arms and transport as they fled. My husband, Michael, who was the American consul in Stanleyville, sifted through the conflicting reports and rumors so that he could send coherent information to the American ambassador in Leopoldville and to the State De-

partment in Washington. Until this Sunday morning the
rebellion had remained for us an indistinct, if menacing,
phantom. And then, in the early hours before dawn,
there appeared a detachment of excited, rag-bag government soldiers. They seized the Congolese sentries
who had been recommended by their own commanders
to guard the American Consulate, pulled one of them
aside, and methodically yet savagely, began to beat
him up.

Michael rushed out to confront the soldiers. I called
to him to come back, but by then he was face to face
with the leader of the government detachment. They
stood talking and gesturing in the glow cast through
the windows by the Consulate lights. The soldiers could
not be calmed. They had, they told Michael, a report
that one of the sentries had taken part in the raid on a
government armory in Stanleyville some weeks before,
in which a quantity of rifles and ammunition had been
stolen.

"We want to question him," their leader said, pointing to the unfortunate sentry. And with that they went
on beating him. The soldiers knew how to mistreat a
prisoner in a way that was painful but did not break his
bones or leave any permanent injury. Michael was unable to pull the man away from them. In a few moments
the soldiers left, still prodding the sentry with their rifle
butts, so that he literally rolled down the driveway
ahead of them like a hoop.

Their departure did not give us any relief. There had

been violence on our doorstep, so to speak, and we felt that it was only a faint suggestion of what might yet come to Stanleyville.

Later that morning Michael drove to the Congolese army headquarters to complain to the commandant, Major Banza, of the violation of Consulate property. The beaten sentry was produced, hobbling, barely able to move.

"It was a mistake," Michael was told.

The poor fellow apparently had been innocent. It was his companion who was the suspected rebel, but being of the same tribal group as the government soldiers, he had been spared a beating. Now he was in prison (after the city's fall, Michael saw him walking about the streets, wearing a rebel uniform). Michael sent the beaten sentry to Dr. Alexander Barlovatz, a Belgian doctor who was a friend of ours.

But this senseless violence had wrenched our life in Stanleyville from its routine, and we knew that it would not settle back to normal. The carefree walks I had taken with Evans, our four-year-old son, along the broad avenues of the city were part of the past. We had looked on the city, since our arrival there, as a cosmopolitan center carved out of the dense forest; one heard French and English in the streets, and European and African mingled in easy familiarity. Abruptly we had been reminded that this was the country of Conrad's *Heart of Darkness*.

Unsettling reports continued to reach us from the

south. It was said that four more Europeans, including two Belgian mining officials and a Catholic priest, had been killed in nearby Maniema Province. If the report was true, that would bring to eight the total of Europeans killed in that province since the revolt had reached there a month before. The wives of many Belgian businessmen had already been sent out of Stanleyville. The Belgian woman who did secretarial work for us had fled the day before the sentries were seized. The American Consulate was left unguarded. Michael asked Major Banza of the Congolese army to send us other sentries, but they never appeared. Rumors flooded in. "The rebels are ten miles from the city." "The army has mutinied." "The president has gone over to the rebels." Michael checked out each rumor, found it to be false or exaggerated, and went on to the next one.

The day after the incident on the lawn, Michael was awakened during the night by a call from a member of his staff who was in touch with the Congolese army. The news was bad. Rebel troops had been seen on the main road leading to Stanleyville from the south. Michael's first thoughts were for Evans and me, since the Consulate was a mile from the center of town.

"I'm going to send you and Evans downtown," he told me. "I'll find a place for you to stay."

I woke up Evans, dressed him and packed a bag. I did not want to leave, but I knew that Michael would feel easier if he did not have to worry about us while he went about his duties. He found a place for us with Phil Mayhew, of the United States Information Service, who had a large apartment in downtown Stanleyville. When I got there I put Evans to bed, then stayed up the remainder of the night trying to contact American missionaries by phone and warn them of the approaching danger. I kept in touch with Michael, too. From my window on the fourth floor I could look down on the street below, where army trucks rumbled past. They were filled with soldiers—the ragtag group, meagerly armed and clothed, which was our last defense against the advancing rebels. The sun came up blood-red over the forest beyond the city.

Later in the morning the news was worse. Confused reports from the south said that a strong rebel force had attacked Wanie Rukula, on the main road forty kilometers from Stanleyville. The last defendable position south of Stanleyville, this town was occupied by a company of government commandos. Michael conferred with François Aradjabu, the Congolese president of the province, and drove downtown to army headquarters to gather what information was available.

"What is the military situation?" Michael asked.

The Congolese colonel said that the rebels were attacking.

"But where are your troops?" Michael persisted. "And where are the rebels?"

The colonel shrugged. *"Je n'en sais rien.* I don't know anything about it."

As the American consul in Stanleyville, Michael was entrusted with the security of American citizens and their interests there. He was now faced with probably the most difficult decision a consul must make: should he ask all American citizens to leave the area? He knew that the rebels had been advancing unchecked through the southern provinces for over a month. At army headquarters he had found only confusion. He felt that he had no alternative. He cabled the American Embassy at Leopoldville to send planes the next morning to evacuate official dependents, nonessential staff members and all of the Americans he could persuade to leave. He also talked to the Embassy over the single-side-band voice radio.

Most of the Americans in the area were missionaries; the bulk of the population of European merchants and businessmen were Belgians. In addition to ourselves and the score of missionaries, there were seven other American government people in Stanleyville: David Grinwis, the vice-consul, Max Kraus and Phil Mayhew of the United States Information Service, communications personnel, Don Parkes, Ernie Houle and Jim Stauffer, and the Consulate's secretary, Joan Allen. There were also a couple of young women tourists living in a downtown apartment and two young conscientious objectors who had been deferred from military service in the United States and had volunteered to work in such distant places as the Protestant University in Stanleyville. That morning Michael called me at the apartment and asked me to visit the home of an American missionary on the outskirts of town. He wanted me to let him know how serious the situation was, and suggest that the missionaries prepare to evacuate their dependents and nonessential people from the city.

The missionary wasn't home when I arrived. His wife and five children were. I explained the reason for my visit, but the woman shook her head.

"It is God's will that we stay," she said.

"I don't see how you can put all the responsibility on God," I told her.

"It is God's will that we stay," she repeated.

Before leaving I suggested that her husband pay a visit to Michael at the Consulate later in the day. That afternoon Alfred Larson, the leader of the Unevangelized Field Missions in the Congo, came to the Consulate as a representative of the local missionaries. Michael explained to him that he was evacuating his own family and the nonessential members of his staff.

"There will be planes enough to evacuate everybody who wants to go," Michael said.

"Are you leaving Stanleyville?" Larson asked.

"No," Michael said. "I will stay with a skeleton staff."

"We cannot leave and see all our property destroyed," he told Michael.

Although one could disagree with their decision, one could not help but admire their courage. The missionaries felt that all of their work would be lost if they deserted their posts now. Michael did not press them further.

There was little for me to do after this but wait. I finished packing, arranging our belongings in two suitcases so that I could take as much as possible with me aboard the plane on Tuesday. Michael and I said little to each other when we were together; neither wanted to mention the fact that I was leaving. I, even less, wanted to mention the fact that he was remaining behind to confront an enemy of which we had heard only the most frightening reports.

I went to the Consulate early the next morning, August 4. The activity there was intense. Under Michael's direction the Consulate staff was preparing to burn the documents and the copies of confidential messages in their files. The men had set up seven metal "destruction barrels" on the lawn, and were stacking the papers that were to be burned in them once Michael gave the order. During the morning Michael learned that Major Harold Asbury, the assistant military attaché at the American Embassy in Leopoldville, was on his way to Stanleyville in a small Embassy plane. The plan was for us to leave on larger planes, which were due in Stanleyville later in the afternoon.

I went about my affairs as if this were simply another day in the long procession of diplomatic workdays. I talked over the arrangements for lunch with Tata Paul, the Consulate cook. The fact that we were not certain how many would be on hand for lunch was not unusual; we had known such uncertainty in other, less extraordinary circumstances. But now every move was made with a certain tension, which increased and intensified when Michael gave the order to destroy the documents and the lawn was ringed with fiercely burning barrels. I had the table set up outside on the terrace, so that he could continue to oversee the destruction during lunch.

The arrangements for lunch were ultimately futile. Late in the morning a small plane buzzed the Consulate. This was the signal which had been set between Michael and Major Asbury, who was announcing his arrival. When Michael saw the plane, he immediately got in his car and drove to the airport. Even then I did not believe there was any need to hurry our preparations for departure. Then the phone rang and it was Michael, calling from the airport. He had been told by the Congolese officers stationed at the airport that the military situation around Stanleyville was hopeless; the officers themselves seemed gripped by pessimism and confusion.

"I'm sending the chauffeur back to pick you and Evans up," Michael said. "Tell Joan Allen to get ready too. I want you to fly to Leo with Major Asbury."

When the chauffeur arrived back at the Consulate, we were waiting on the lawn with our suitcases. We said our good-byes, the staff helped load our suitcases into the car, and in a moment we were on our way to the airport.

There, away from the apparent security of the American Consulate and downtown Stanleyville, we were enveloped by the confusion of war. Congolese soldiers, stripped to the waist, milled around us. The voices, the expressions, the gestures of the people we saw seemed without purpose. Michael was on the landing strip, talking to Major Asbury. We saw, just beyond them, the twin-engine Beechcraft that was to take us to Leopoldville. I learned that I would be allowed to bring only one suitcase with me in the little plane, which was heavily loaded. Michael took the other suitcase out of my hand, and I hurriedly shifted a few essential items for Evans into the bag I could take.

"Do a little reconnaissance for us if you can," Michael told Major Asbury. "We just don't have any hard reports on the rebels around here. If you spot anything, let me know."

Major Asbury nodded. "I'll find out what I can," he said, and then he looked at me. "Don't worry about Jo. I'll take care of her too."

I kissed Michael good-bye. "Don't be a hero," I told him. "Come back to me."

Major Asbury helped me aboard, where I joined Evans and Joan Allen in the little cabin. As I looked back through the door, I saw Michael walking toward the car, carrying my other suitcase. The car, with its American and consular flags flying from the slender rods on its fenders, looked very gay and brave.

The plane roared down the runway and left the ground. Major Asbury was already in contact with Michael, who had gone to the airport's control tower. We dipped low over the new airstrip east of the city and saw a file of trucks moving toward it (this later proved to have been the advance guard of the rebel forces). Major Asbury reported to Michael on what he had seen and then turned the plane south toward Leopoldville. The dim matter-of-fact voice in which Michael acknowledged Major Asbury's information suddenly altered.

"Bye, bye, baby doll," he called. And then we were on our way.

Joan Allen and I were still in a state which must have been something close to shock, but Evans, inspecting the plane in the manner of any healthy four-year-old, seemed happily unaware of the gathering disaster below us. Then abruptly he turned and looked up at me.

"Will they tie me up and throw me out of the airplane?" he asked.

For a moment I didn't understand him. Then I remembered. Only a week before, while Evans was playing on the floor nearby, a group of us had been talking about Patrice Lumumba, the Congo's former prime minister who had been assassinated in 1960. It was said at the time that he had been bound hand and foot and tossed from the plane by his captors when he had reached his destination.

. . .

Two hours after we left Stanleyville the rebels entered the city. When I reached the American Embassy in Leopoldville, I learned that the ambassador had already received cables from Michael, describing the battle for the city. He was still in contact with the outside world. The two USIS men, Kraus and Mayhew, had been evacuated on a later plane, but the Consulate staff, composed of Grinwis, Houle, Stauffer and Parkes, were still with Michael. Houle and Parkes, who had been scheduled for evacuation, had not been able to get to the airport in the afternoon because of the fighting in the city.

At six-fifteen that evening another cable arrived. The Congolese army, Michael said, was advancing across the lawn, apparently pushing the rebels back. Eight minutes later he cabled again, reporting that Congolese troops were moving rapidly and in numbers away from the Consulate, pushing the rebels back from the south. If the situation continued to improve, he said, he would not abandon the Consulate "due to psychological effect."

He cabled again almost immediately: POLE SHOT AND ROPE CUT BY GUNFIRE BUT CONSULATE FLAG STILL FLYING.

Fifteen minutes later we learned that the airport, under heavy fire, was preparing to shut down. Stanleyville was effectively cut off from the outside world. The city had been engulfed by the doped and vengeful Simbas of the rebel army.

2 ★
In the Beginning

It was not purely by chance that Michael and I, Midwestern Americans by birth, the parents of four growing children, and hardly the adventurous type, found ourselves in the heart of this savage African war. Almost from childhood Michael had pointed toward a career that would take him overseas. The son of a prominent nuclear physicist at the University of Chicago, he had accompanied his parents abroad on a number of trips during which his father had put himself in touch with the leading atomic physicists of prewar Europe. Swiss farms and French railway carriages form a part of his earliest memories. My summer trips were not as extensive, but they seemed exotic to a girl growing up in Boonville, Indiana. Our summer home was in New Mexico, and deserts, Indians and spectacular sunsets were the glories of my girlhood.

The unfathomable world of nuclear physics brought Michael and me together. New Mexico is famous for the atomic laboratories of Los Alamos, as well as for its Indians and deserts. It was there that Michael's father came to work after almost twenty years at the University of Chicago. My sister knew the Hoyts, and through her I met Michael, who had come home briefly on leave from the Air Force. When he left the United States for duty in Korea, I still knew him only as a family friend. I saw his mother occasionally, and she urged me to write to him, as mothers always want others to write to their boys overseas. I did, and also sent him cookies and other presents. Michael wrote back to thank me. We kept in touch. And then suddenly Michael was home again and I knew he was something more than a family friend.

The Air Force sent Michael to Mobile, Alabama. When he wrote to me, asking me to fly there and marry him, I came. Our future was terribly indefinite. Though we both intended to go back to school, I was marrying at the time an Air Force sergeant who eventually would return to civilian life when he had discharged his obligations to his country. Michael obtained a two-day pass and we drove across the state border to Lucedale, Mississippi, which offered impatient couples the immediate issuance of a marriage license.

After we had located the courthouse, we signed the necessary papers and paid for the license. A couple of those people who seem to hang around courthouses just for that purpose consented to serve as the official witnesses of our ceremony. The sheriff led us into a pleasantly soft room, with many books on its stained wooden shelves, a couple of oriental rugs and a long library table. He closed the door, said "Let us begin," and then opened the ceremony at the top of his voice, nearly deafening us.

Michael had changed into civilian clothes for our wedding. I wore something blue, but what, I cannot remember. We had bought an inexpensive silver Navaho ring with a tiny turquoise. At the appropriate moment Michael tried to slip it on my finger, and found it, predictably, too small. With my help he jammed it on, and I have worn it ever since. Then we completed our vows and drove back to Mobile for our brief honeymoon.

Our early life together was typical of the transient lives led by young people who are temporarily tied to the armed services. At first we rented a second-floor apartment in an old Mobile mansion. The owner turned out to be an alcoholic, and his wife a drug addict. When my father came to Mobile to visit us, he was horrified, not so much by the moral climate as by our physical surroundings. The building was tumble-down, an obvious firetrap, and one stairway had been blocked off by the owners.

"What will you do in case there's a fire?" my father asked us.

There was, we suddenly realized, no answer. My father solved the problem by buying us a trailer. The only difficulty was that the trailer happened to be in Indiana. On Michael's next leave we drove north to pick it up, fully intending to haul it back to Alabama with us. We were quite proud of our new home. It was thirty-seven and a half feet long and completely furnished. When I told the salesman I didn't like the curtains and bedspreads, he offered us other patterns from which to choose. We ordered the special lights and brakes a car requires to haul a trailer and had them installed. Then, with the salesman at the wheel, we headed south out of town. We were halfway up a steep hill when he stopped the car, shook hands pleasantly with Michael, and stepped out, wishing us luck. The trailer loomed behind us like some ominous monster. We managed to guide it to the nearest gas station before the sense of our inadequacy completely overcame us.

"Back it up, buddy," the station attendant told Michael. "Move it back to that other pump."

"But I can't back this thing up," Michael said helplessly.

"Just do what I tell you," the attendant said matter-of-factly.

Michael, one eye on the attendant and the other on the row of gas pumps, gingerly backed the trailer into the designated position. We had managed the first hurdle with only a small dent in the roof. After filling the gas tank we set off again, at twenty-five miles an hour but with a distinct sensation that we were traveling ninety. Finally, exhausted, we pulled off the highway. There, despite the four neat beds in that great trailer behind us, we curled up in the front seat of the car and fell asleep.

By the time we arrived in Boonville, Indiana, we had conceded defeat. We left the car and the trailer at the bottom of a hill (every hill had become a nightmare to us!) and walked up to my sister's house. There it was agreed in family conference that we would unhitch the trailer and drive back to Mobile unencumbered, while my brother, who was accustomed to driving heavy trucks and machinery, would follow us in his own car with the trailer.

When Michael's tour of duty with the Air Force finally came to an end in 1955, we decided that he should return to school and get his master's degree. He chose to attend the University of Illinois at Champaign-Urbana. There I found a half-acre of land, which we rented from a retired postman, and set up our trailer (this time having had the foresight to hire a man to drive it north for us). But a single trailer was no longer adequate for our needs. There were three children by this time, two sons, Reed and Phelps, and a three-month-old daughter named Scot (we have tried to find names for our children that cannot be shortened or distorted into "cute" nicknames). To solve the problem, my brother found another trailer in Chicago and sent it down to us. When it arrived we simply attached it to our old one, first removing its wheels to avoid being classed as a "trailer park" and taxed accordingly.

Mr. Romney, the man from whom we rented the land, installed a water pipe and a cesspool for us, and hooked up our trailers to his electricity. A trifle giddy, perhaps, with our own half-acre of land after all those years in cramped quarters, we set out to farm a part of it. Michael drove to town one day and bought forty tomato plants; later the same day I drove to town, unaware that he had been there, and bought fifty tomato plants. Every one of them, perversely, flourished, and we and our university friends, in self-defense, gorged ourselves on tomatoes for the rest of the summer. To our boundless surprise, our sweet corn and cabbages thrived as well.

What, the reader may ask, has all this to do with life in the Foreign Service? While we were living, we were learning. The one big lesson I learned from living in a trailer was that one must stay organized. This may be commonplace advice to the novice housewife, but the demands that the restricted space in a trailer makes upon one brings the lesson home in a rather special way. We had real "togetherness" during those years, and it could very quickly have deteriorated into chaos under those conditions. I learned by exacting experience how to order and organize a house under difficult circumstances, and there is nothing I can think of that would have better prepared me for the life of a Foreign Service wife.

By this time I was aware that if all went well with Michael's application, the Foreign Service was to be my destiny. While still busy with his graduate courses in history at Illinois, Michael had applied to take the exam-

ination for a commission as a United States Foreign
Service officer. These men are the career professionals
who perform the chief work of the State Department at
home and overseas. Michael could imagine no other career which promised such lifelong satisfaction: the opportunity to live in far, strange places, to meet and work
with all kinds of people, to perform interesting work,
and, at the same time, to do something meaningful
while serving his country. It is important for a woman to
know that her husband earns satisfaction as well as a
living from his career; further, it is exciting for *her* to be
able to share in his work. That, for me, was one of the
most provocative aspects of the Foreign Service—that I
would play a crucial part in Michael's success or failure.

The closing months of Michael's academic life were
enlivened by a sense of the challenge that confronted
us. He took the State Department's intensive day-long
examination, and we waited anxiously to learn how he
had done. It was two months before we heard: Michael
had passed! But the most harrowing moment still lay
ahead of us. In March, 1956, Michael, Reed and I (we
left the two younger children at home with my sister) went to Chicago, where he was to face the oral examination. A board, consisting of veteran State Department officials, travels around the country giving the
exam at convenient locations. The questions are varied,
ranging from an intensive examination of the applicant
in the field in which he has indicated his special interests
lie, to a discussion of the applicant's working knowl-

edge of politics, history and the liberal arts. Often "trick" questions are asked to test the applicant's reactions under stress. The applicant who tries to get by on his glibness is apt to be undone by the knowledgeable examiners. It is the kind of ordeal which must make even the most well-informed young person approach it with considerable uneasiness. Yet I think I was more nervous than Michael.

I wished him good luck. Reed and I walked over to the Field Museum to while away the hour or so until we were to meet Michael on the museum's front steps. Reed was fascinated by the exhibits; I don't remember a thing I saw. It seemed to me that we had walked miles and miles when I noticed that the hour was up. I took Reed by the hand and hurried to the main entrance. Just as we arrived I saw Michael bounding up the museum steps. I didn't have to ask how he had done. It was all right there—on his grinning face.

Apparently he had done beautifully. Immediately after the examination a member of the board told him he had passed, and would be appointed to the Foreign Service following a medical examination and an exhaustive security check into his and, I learned later, my backgrounds. Three months later he completed the work for his master's degree in modern European history at the University of Illinois. Within a few days his orders arrived from the State Department. He was to report to Washington for a three-month period of training. We gave away the two trailers—one to my brother and the other to my nephew—packed our bags and, with Reed, Phelps and Scot in tow, made the first of a great many trips as a Foreign Service family.

We moved into a furnished apartment in Falls Church, Virginia. Michael was sworn in as a Foreign Service officer of the lowest grade and began his classes at the Foreign Service Institute. Since he had just completed one grueling year of studies, he was a little disheartened to learn that the original "three-month course" at the Institute would be extended, at least several times over. In addition to the general course for young diplomats, Michael was required to take an intensive three-month course in French. He had spoken French fluently as a child on his trips to Switzerland, and had studied it again in high school. Now most of it was forgotten. Only the accent returned easily, as he struggled with vocabularies and verb forms.

Even less familiar was his next course: a three-month indoctrination in government budget, fiscal and disbursing operations. Ordinarily, Foreign Service officers are not assigned to accounting duties. However, at the time there was a desperate shortage of accountants for our overseas posts. The State Department, casting about for a temporary solution to its problems, decided to draw on the newly appointed officers, put them through a crash course, and hopefully send them out to keep the books in its embassies and consulates throughout the world. Michael, who could not balance a checkbook, was chosen to become such an expert. He struggled manfully, and I am able to testify today that Michael *did* learn to balance a checkbook.

And it was also my turn to go back to school. A young Foreign Service officer's wife is asked to take a two-week indoctrination course at the Institute before going overseas with her husband. My mother came east to look after the children, while I set off on my first round of courses. There was a class in American history, which probably should be emphasized more than it is, and a class in managing servants, which undoubtedly could be done away with; one learns to play these matters by ear. Diplomats came before us to explain what the Foreign Service was, and to go into their specialties in some detail. Foreign Service officers, we were told, were the "shock troops" of the Cold War. From the lowest ranking officer in a remote consulate to the career ambassador in a vital European capital, they conducted the diplomatic and consular affairs of the United States. Besides an outline of the many duties our husbands would be asked to undertake as the representatives of our country abroad, there was some very practical advice for us. The wife of a prominent United States ambassador remained for a question-and-answer period after her lecture.

"How many sets of wineglasses is it necessary for us to buy when we're preparing for an overseas assignment?" one young wife asked.

"Honey," the ambassador's wife said, "you can get

by with cheese glasses if you want to. Just as long as there's booze in them, they'll drink it."

Properly enlightened, I waited impatiently with Michael for our first assignment. Finally his orders arrived. Michael was to report to Karachi, Pakistan, as the third secretary and "accounting assistant" in the Budget and Fiscal section of the American Embassy.

3 ★
En Voyage

It was at this point that the unusual experience I had acquired in organizing our trailer began to pay dividends in our lives. We had only three weeks' notice before leaving the United States. Most of our relatives had visited us in Washington within recent months so that there was no necessity for us to set off on a round of farewells, and this was a blessing. Now, in the spring of 1957, I had to prepare three small children, as well as Michael and myself, for the unimaginable changes we would face in establishing a new home on the Asian subcontinent. At that time there were few things available locally which we regarded as the essentials of life. For Reed, who was six years old and in the first grade, there was the prospect of transferring to an entirely different school system. For Phelps, who was two and a half, and Scot, one and a half, there was the equally difficult prospect of growing to awareness among foreign people and landscapes.

With time growing short, my first concern was how to transfer and set up a home—in its physical sense—in a strange city halfway around the world. The Foreign Service, itself, helped me over the first step. Wives who have been assigned to overseas posts may call the Geographic Bureau in the State Department responsible for that area of the world, and ask to be put in touch with someone who has just returned to the United States from the post in question. I was given the phone number of a woman who had arrived in Washington after several years in Karachi. I called her and we chatted for almost an hour. By the time we hung up I had enough information to start me off on an expensive yet indispensable round of shopping.

First I stocked up on clothing. Short pants for the boys were a necessity. And shoes. I bought three sets of shoes for each child, the second set a half-size larger than the first, and the third set a half-size larger still; then I left orders at the store for shoes to be shipped to us in steadily increasing sizes at regular intervals during our two-year assignment in Karachi.

For Michael I bought plenty of wash-and-wear suits. The few dry-cleaning establishments in Karachi, I had been told, were not very efficient, and suits were generally returned to their owners considerably smaller and more faded than when they had been sent. For myself I bought plenty of cotton dresses—*short* cottons, for there was to be a great deal of outdoor entertaining in Karachi, and the local insects find havens along the hems of trailing evening dresses.

We already knew that the American Embassy would provide us with a furnished house in Karachi. The furnishings, however, would be limited to "furniture," and today an American family that includes three young children can hardly be expected to get along without its electrical appliances. They were next on my shopping list. A washing machine, for instance. It would have to be a wringer-type machine, for we were told that Karachi lacked the water pressure to make an automatic model function. Besides, the workmen would not know how to fix one if anything went wrong with it. We would need a freezer, as well as the refrigerator provided for us by the Embassy, if we hoped to vary our menus at all in Karachi, for vegetables were sold there only in season.

Each step uncovered a further problem. The appliances I ordered had to conform to the 220-volt system they would operate on in Pakistan, rather than the 110 volts almost exclusively used here in the United States. Transformers, it is true, can be used with some appliances to convert them to the 220-volt system, but they are cumbersome and expensive. Another problem I thought I had prepared myself for was the type of electric light bulbs sold in Pakistan. There I would find only bulbs with a bayonet base, so I had been told to bring a supply of bulbs to fit my lamps. Dutifully, I bought screw-in bulbs, specifying that they were to be "220's" (but when I arrived in Karachi I learned that the store had sold me bulbs which would operate only on 110 volts, and I was obliged to use transformers to get my lamps to work).

And there was the problem of an automobile. Here again we had to be careful. Automatic shifts were, we learned, difficult to get serviced in Pakistan at the time. Our own Chevy had an automatic drive, but after buying all the appliances and other supplies, we discovered we could not afford a new car. So we shipped the Chevy, and hoped for the best.

Then I turned my attention to the smaller items. There were certain articles of food which we had been told to bring with us—powdered milk, for instance, and sugar and seasonings, all of which were difficult to buy in Karachi. We bought cases of toilet paper and cartons of Kleenex. Most important of all were the medicines and other items from the drug store. I filled a foot locker with what I imagined to be a three-month supply, and asked a local druggist to ship other medicines to me in Karachi. I knew we would need Kaopectate, as well as bug repellent, bandages, antiseptic soaps and iodine (the tiniest cut is liable to fester and cause endless trouble in that climate).

We left at the end of May. I had broken up our provisions, taking some of the most essential items with us, shipping others by air freight and hoping they would arrive before we did. We presented ourselves at the

Washington airport in high spirits. The trip itself was something of a nightmare: forty-four hours in a propeller-driven plane to Karachi, and three restless children clambering on and off my lap. There were frequent stops —Gander, London, Paris, Munich. At London, where we ate our breakfast at five o'clock in the morning in the quiet airport dining room, Phelps dropped his eggs sunny side up on the red carpet, much to the discomfort of a very proper waiter.

It was midnight when we landed at Beirut. There we were asked to leave the plane while it was cleaned by a ground crew. I roused the children, who were grumpy, but not nearly so grumpy, we found, as the customs men who had to rouse themselves at that hour to check our passports. It was my first indication that Americans are not treated overseas as courteously as we are accustomed to being treated by travel and official people at home in the United States. Our passports were taken brusquely from us and we were told sternly, it seemed to us, to stand "over there" and wait. Far more upsetting than the customs people, however, was a drunken American businessman, who pestered us at the bar to which we had all been herded. He insisted that we have a drink with him—what he wanted to force on us, I don't remember, but it was some uninviting local absinthe-like milky concoction. We declined. The pest persisted, and I grew very uncomfortable. Suddenly, blessed relief appeared in the person of a young Lebanese woman who worked at the airport.

"Would you like to get back on the plane with the children?" she asked me.

I would, and did, thanking her profusely. Our plane took off after a long delay and started on the last leg of its journey. At dawn we looked down on a desolate landscape, an eternity of desert, apparently devoid of any living thing, the coastline of the Arabian Sea and the desert that flowed into it. There was sand and hills and clay, all swept by a hostile wind. That this was the approach to the city in which we were to spend the next two years was a disquieting thought.

Someone on the plane detected Karachi in the distance. The land now reminded me of the Southwest I had known since girlhood—the bare red sand hills, the earth-colored buildings looking from the air like the adobe homes of New Mexico Indians—and I was somewhat comforted. The strangeness would not be overwhelming. I changed the children into the clothes I had saved for our arrival and freshened myself up as well as possible.

The plane circled the city and came in for its landing. We drew up in front of the terminal and the engines stopped, but still we could not leave our seats. We were about to be disinfected, we learned, with a bug bomb. We sat in the incredible heat of that airless cabin, enduring a mounting impatience. The children moaned and sniffled. Then suddenly the cabin door was thrown open for us and we stepped out into the blinding sun of an Asian city.

It was as if a blanket of burning cotton had been dropped over us. We gasped in the heat. Then, miraculously it seemed, we saw a couple of friendly faces.

"Are you the Hoyts?" one of them asked.

We said that we were. The friendly man who had spoken identified himself as Herb Griffin, Michael's boss in the Embassy, and then introduced his wife. They helped us into the terminal, which was somewhat cooler than outside. The Griffins had come to meet us, smoothing our way through customs and pointing us toward a temporary house. There was, we learned, a "transient" house, maintained by the Embassy for families such as ours, and stocked in advance by wives of our colleagues with boiled water, tinned soups, milk, clean sheets and the other necessities which would carry us over the first few days at our new post.

But better even than the house (it came complete with servants!) were the welcoming words of the Griffins and the other people with whom Michael would be working. Here, at the very beginning, the East dropped a little of its strangeness because of the kindness which helped us ease into a new and fascinating world.

4 ★
*First Post**

Karachi, we had to be told, and told again, had been honored not many years past as one of the most modern cities in the East. If one looked closely, one could detect the skeleton of that small model city, engulfed now by an unmanageable metropolis we stared at through the car windows as we were driven to our temporary quarters in the spring of 1957.

It has had a curious history. Apparently, founded in the early eighteenth century, Karachi remained an unimportant town until the British, expanding their claims

---

* This section describes a Karachi of another day. Following a bloodless coup, the administration of President Mohammed Ayub Khan built refugee resettlement camps, cleaned and drained the buffalo wallows, moved the livestock to outlying areas, and abolished the pedicab as a form of inhuman servitude. Much of the population pressure was also taken off Karachi by the new regime's decision to move the capital to a modern, planned city, Islamabad, now abuilding on the beautiful Plains of Potwar north of Rawalpindi in the Punjab.

in India during the next century, cast about for a suitable seaport on the Arabian Sea to supply the rich agricultural Punjab and open the way into the vital Northwest Frontier. Their choice fell on Karachi. British planners laid out an attractive and efficient city, developed its port facilities and supervised its growth. The city prospered. During World War II it was a major entry point for the military supplies poured into India by the Allies.

Independence changed everything. When Pakistan broke away from India to set up its separate government in 1947, Karachi was chosen as its capital. (The capital has since been shifted to Rawalpindi.) Savage fighting broke out between the Pakistanis and the Indians. Moslem refugees streamed across the border into Pakistan from India, which was predominantly Hindu. The goal of many of these displaced persons was the urban concentration of the new nation. Karachi suddenly found itself inundated by hundreds of thousands of refugees. The population increased tenfold. On Karachi's outskirts there grew crowded refugee camps, with people making use of everything they could lay their hands on to put shelters together. When they ran out of building material, they literally burrowed into the mud of the river delta. Pakistan's weak and corrupt governments could do little to resettle these unfortunate people, and hardly more to provide them with the necessary municipal services. Electricity, water supplies, hospitals and food were hopelessly inadequate in the face of the inflated population. Somehow, out of the mudholes and refugee camps, a few people pulled themselves up to form a sort of *nouveau riche* class. These people wanted better homes and facilities. And so all around us, when we started our new life in Karachi, we saw evidence of the tremendous building boom that was both transforming and choking the city, as thousands of other people entered into new lives of their own.

Fortunately, the problem of a home for the Hoyt family was solved by the American Embassy there. I don't mean to say that we were to live in one of those "Little Americas" in which Americans are so often quarantined from the day-to-day life of the country in which they are stationed. After we had lived for several months in our transient quarters, the Embassy assigned us to one of their houses in a residential section of Karachi. The house next door was occupied by two families, one Pakistani, one Dutch. Across the street were Pakistanis, and a little further down the street lived an American businessman.

Ours was a pleasant house, much newer than it might have looked to a stranger, since the cinder blocks of which it was constructed were held together by a poor grade of cement, and the stuff tended to crumble under the elements and even under one's touch. (Wood was seldom used there in building because what little might be available in the scrubby countryside would surely be infested by insects.) The inside of the house was coated with whitewash, also of a poor quality. The "painters" who descended on us took eight or nine days to do the job, and by the time they had completed the whole, the living room, which they had worked on first, had already begun to peel. I stood my ground at this point, ordering them to repaint the living room even if they had to remain through the night. I was grateful in one sense, however, for the weakness of their whitewash solution. Because the painting crew had slopped it on the walls with flabby contraptions which reminded me of dish mops, they left an awful mess in their wake. Yet when we cleaned it up, we found it came off the floors as easily as if it had been milk.

The house itself had four bedrooms, two bathrooms, a combined living and dining room area and a large screened porch in which we tended to spend most of our time. The living room was round, a shape which supposedly invests a house with good luck, but which I found devilishly hard to furnish. For closets there were big wooden boxlike structures called Elmiras, which swallowed up our belongings but at the same time dominated the rooms in which they stood. The long narrow bathrooms were provided with terrazzo tubs, seven feet long and terribly narrow.

The kitchen was archaic. There was a charcoal stove, an oil stove and a water container in one section, an icebox and a tiny sink in the other. A wall between converted what was a small space into two hot and airless cubbyholes. I was told that the reason for this arrangement was that in Pakistani houses the cook-bearer, who washes the dishes, and the second boy, who takes care of the pots and pans, must be separated in order to keep them from being at each other's throats all day. In the popular view, they are instinctive foes, like the cobra and the mongoose.

Outside was a walled compound in which the children played, and a garden, presided over by a competent *mali,* or gardener. There were vines on the wall, blooming straw flowers, two palm trees, a hibiscus and a flamboyant Christmas plant which produced orange flowers and orange and yellow leaves. The garden, like so much of the Pakistani countryside, reminded me of New Mexico, and I was very content there.

We had more servants than rooms. At one time I counted ten servants in our house, varying in their skills and usefulness. There was a cook-bearer, or number one boy, followed by the *hamal,* or number two boy. The faces blur, the duties seem all mixed up in my memory, but the rest of the line-up (which would have taken a Casey Stengel to manage) included an *ayah,* or nanny; a *dhobi,* or washer man; the aforementioned *mali;* a *dhersi,* or sewing man; a sweeper; and a *chowkidar.* This last functionary was a night watchman, whose salary was paid by the Embassy. He was a necessity in Karachi, even though the windows of our house were barred. The bars were not of the sturdiest kind and could be wrenched away by a muscular burglar. There had, in fact, been a number of burglaries in our area. The enlarged population of the city could not find suf-

ficient employment, and its rich residential areas, therefore, attracted the desperate. One American family had
lost practically all of its belongings when a thorough-
going gang backed a truck up to the front door while all
of them were away one night and took every item that
could be squeezed into it. We plied our night watchman
with coffee, and it is probable that he spent at least part
of the night reasonably awake.

Today's ordinary American housewife cannot imagine the scope of the servant problem in underdeveloped
areas. Labor is cheaper than gadgets, and one comes to
depend so much on hired hands that these people's per-
sonalities and problems occupy an inordinate amount of
one's waking hours. To open one's door to a staff of servants is to open a book on a whole world of love and hate,
vice and virtue, happiness and tragedy. Our home in
Karachi seemed large enough to encompass them all.

Soon after we set up housekeeping in Karachi, we suspected that our first crew of trusted servants was steal-
ing everything that wasn't nailed down. Part of it was
my fault; I left the food cabinets unlocked. I began to
miss a few objects here and there. One day, while the
servants were off, I decided to play detective. I poked
around in their quarters, which were over a "garage" in
back of the house. I found all sorts of tinned goods and
household knickknacks.

When the servants returned the next day, I called
them all together. Putting on as stern a face as I could, I
ordered them to return what they had stolen. At first

they denied all. There were avowals of innocence and tears of indignation. I persisted. Then, reluctantly, they began to drag things out of hiding. Their cache was immense. I had had no idea until that moment how much they had really made off with. Food, silver, Michael's clothing—they were all there.

I fired the culprits on the spot. Not without a feeling of guilt, I must admit, because even in those early days in the city I had already had an opportunity to see for myself the utter poverty in which so many Pakistanis spent their lives. It was heartbreaking, yet at the same time I was a woman trying to establish a home for her family in a foreign land and I needed some defenses; otherwise, I would have watched our home dissolve.

I managed to find another staff of servants, ones who seemed to us to be models of honesty (although after we left Karachi and they went to work for friends of ours, these servants walked off with half their household belongings). Perhaps I had learned my lesson well, and thereafter exposed them to few temptations. I kept under lock and key our food and whatever else could be carried away. And a friend of mine, who had been some time in Karachi, offered me another bit of advice.

"When you pick up a small object like an ashtray," she said, "always be sure that you put it back exactly where you took it from. If objects don't have a special spot in the room, you will find that little by little they will be edged toward the door, and one day you'll find that they have gone out the door for good."

It was with more regret that we lost our first *ayah*. She was a young girl, pretty, friendly and alert. We congratulated ourselves on having found just the right sort of girl to take care of our young children. As a precautionary measure, we took her to the hospital for a checkup. It was the usual thing: chest x-rays, blood tests, and so forth. Then the report came back to us. Our *ayah* had syphilis!

I hated to give her up. "Can't you give her some shots and clear it up?" I asked the doctor.

"Forget it," he said, shaking his head. "*This* one will pick it up again next week."

We did have our share of amorous servants, and the problem extended to what the English call "dalliance below stairs." To prevent our home from deteriorating into some sort of disorderly house, we had to sack two other servants, a man and a woman. A couple of days later we had a letter from the man, obviously dictated to a professional letter-writer in the market place. It read, in part:

> Respected Sir:
> While employed in your service, your ayah took a loan of Rs. 80 from me in a piecemeal way. Whenever I demanded her the repayment of money, she always wanted me to intercourse with her, for which I never agreed.
> In the night of 26th instant when you had been out, I arranged your bed, etc., and later on came to keep water in the bathroom for your bathing. The ayah was sitting on her bed. The children were asleep. The ayah

called me but I said to her that I am busy hence cannot listen towards her. However on her repeated calling I came to her and asked what she wanted to say. She forced me to intercourse with her but I did not. On which she said that once before I have been warned by her for not doing intercourse and if I do not do so she will get me thrown out of employment by reporting a false complaint to your honour. After completing my work I left the bungalow for my quarter. On the next day she through another bearer got reported the matter to your honour falsely saying that I illegally intercoursed with her.

Sir, may I courage to state that the ayah is of corrupted nature and she had been doing such things with other employees too.

However I do not mind of termination of services, but request you kindly to repay the loan of Rs. 80 taken by your ayah. Otherwise I will be compelled to file a suit in the civil court case against you and the ayah, which please note.

We did not hear any more from the fellow, nor from his lawyer, and the case sputtered out. Thankfully, most of our servants were good people, hard-working and anxious to please. They generally came to us in a haphazard way. The Karachi "employment agency" was very informal. You simply told your head boy what you were looking for, and when he went to the market place he passed the word around. The next morning we would look out the window to see the applicants for the job queuing up outside our front door.

The children, of course, began to pick up bits and pieces of the local language (which was Urdu) much more rapidly than we did. This was chiefly because of their close association with the servants. There was a mutual understanding between them of the kind which is difficult to achieve between adults of different races. We still recall many of these people with affection. Scot, in particular, had as a favorite the *ayah* we finally settled on, an old woman who had been raised as a Roman Catholic and who spoke excellent English. She used to read to Scot in the evenings.

In general, the servants approved of everything the children did although when Reed reached the stage when he thought he could earn a little money by watering the grass, the yard boy became very upset.

"The *sahib* isn't supposed to *do* anything," he kept insisting.

At times, however, the servants grew a little too helpful. One day an *ayah* we had in our employ appeared for work with her hands and feet colored a deep red; she had dyed them, as a beauty aid, with henna. We simply shrugged it off, being pleased that she was pleased with herself.

That night, however, she decided that the children would sleep better if she applied the henna treatment to them. She coated Scot's hands and feet, then turned her attention to Reed. That was when we were alerted to the matter. Reed set up an awful howl, having been half asleep before the *ayah* began to work on him, and unsure of what was going on. I ran into his bedroom to find henna smeared over his sheets and even on parts of the wall. I let the *ayah* know, despite the language barrier, that I was very unhappy about the whole affair, and I am sure that she understood. Poor Scot was an apparition in her henna-ed hands and feet, but I could not see that it helped her to sleep any better.

5 ★

We Settle Down

But we had to extricate ourselves from our servants and their problems if we were to live our own lives in Karachi, just as we must extricate our narrative from them if it is to proceed. We had been set down in a strange world, and obliged to make the most of it. By confronting and overcoming the problems of daily life there, each of us was enormously enriched.

For the children the transition had its special difficulties. It was not easy for them to be confined continually to the walled compound behind the house, but a number of unpleasant incidents which had occurred in the neighborhood made it advisable to keep them from roaming about on their own. Under normal conditions (but nothing is normal when one's environment is so strange) we might not have bothered with an *ayah* to care for the children. Most foreign families in Karachi, however, hired one to keep an eye on their children because it was not unknown for a little girl there to be raped by a male servant. But there were compensations even in the compound. One of them was the man who toured the neighborhood with a pair of monkeys. For one rupee (about twenty-one cents) he would stage a half-hour show for the children, and they never seemed to tire of it.

Despite the occasional restrictions on all of us, we began to feel alive in Karachi in a way that one seldom does in the bland and antiseptic atmosphere we had left behind us. There were new experiences, new sensations. One of the principal items in our Karachi diet was buffalo meat; soaked overnight and cooked long enough, it made a distinctive and rather pleasant dish. Happily, we were obliged to bake our own bread. The bread one bought in the market was apt to be full of bugs and was very poor. But all of the servants seemed to know how to make excellent bread with the flour we imported, and the steamy little kitchen was often relieved by the wonderful smell of baking yeast loaves. This bread was truly delicious. The children even today dislike what they call the "squishy" product that the big American baking firms pass off on the public as bread.

In fact, there were very few of their accustomed staples and "goodies" that the children could consume in Karachi. The milk was powdered (after drinking powdered milk abroad for all these years, the children have no taste for "real" milk and so they seldom drink it when they return to the United States). The ice cream in Karachi was inedible, the Cokes were sickeningly sweet. So the children, in a sense, grew up on such exotic dishes as buffalo meat and the "hot" curry dishes of the Middle East. Scot came to love rice curry, and one of my most vivid memories of that time is of Scot picking up her rice with a torn-off piece of *japati*, an unleavened bread which is shaped like a pancake, just as she had seen the Pakistanis do.

We sent Reed, the only one of our children then old enough, to the Karachi Grammar School. It was a private school, presided over by a headmaster of the old-fashioned, strict variety who had been imported for the purpose from England. Another school there was reported to be very "social," and we thought it best to place Reed where the emphasis was on learning. He had difficulty at first, but a friend of ours in the American Embassy tutored him for a time, and soon he caught up with the other students.

We were all becoming Karachi "veterans." Perhaps it was superficially most noticeable in me, since I tan so deeply that several Pakistani friends asked me, after I had been in the sun for a while, if I was an "American Indian." There was a joke then current in Karachi about how one could judge the length of time a Westerner had been there: if a newcomer found a fly in his beer, he sent back the beer; if he had been there for a while, he simply removed the fly and drank the beer; but if he had been there a long time, he removed the fly, held it over the glass and squeezed it, then drank the beer.

We never got quite that far, but we did pick up some useful hints about making our way through life in Karachi. One of the most useful for dining out was passed along to us by our Embassy doctor. Rice, of course, was a feature of almost every Pakistani meal. The doctor advised us not to scrape a spoonful haphazardly from the rice that was set out on buffet tables. Because Pakistani homes at that time were scarcely ever equipped with screens, the flies had free entry and invariably congregated on the exposed mounds of rice. The trick, we learned, was to fumble around with the rice as if we were mixing it up, while in truth we were scraping off the fly-encrusted outer edges and extracting a portion from the interior of the mound.

Another emblem of the veteran in Karachi was, especially in a woman's case, faded clothes. Because of the heat, cotton dresses had to be washed out after every use. Soon I found that my cottons were beginning to fade, but nobody really noticed because theirs looked exactly the same. And because of all the outdoor entertaining, one's heels, habitually sunken in the grass of somebody's lawn, began to take on a greenish cast.

Since Michael's appointment to the American Embassy was the reason for our being in Karachi in the first place, our lives really revolved about his. He worked in the Embassy accounting department. Although it was his first overseas post and he was in a very junior capacity there, he supervised the work of several locally hired employees, helping to keep the Embassy accounts, overseeing current disbursements and budgeting for future expenditures.

If on the surface Michael's duties resembled those of an accountant, there occasionally came his way certain duties which took him out of a humdrum routine. Sometimes he was called upon to take the place of another officer who was ill or on leave. Perhaps the most bizarre of these duties sent him to Lahore, a city in western Punjab. An eighty-two-year-old American woman, who was living with her son there, had died. In the absence of the regular consular officer, Michael was asked to make the arrangements for the complicated process of having the body shipped back to the United States. In that climate bodies are usually not kept long enough to require the services of an embalmer, and Michael discovered that there was only one qualified embalmer in all of West Pakistan, and he was located in Karachi, where the body was taken.

When the body had been prepared and placed in a suitable casket, Michael learned that the woman's son wanted to accompany the body back to the United States by plane. Michael contacted the airlines, gave them the measurements of the casket, and was assured that it could be accommodated aboard the flight on which the son had made his reservations. Michael and I drove to the Karachi airport to make certain it went aboard the outgoing plane without any complica-

tions. But complications there were! For forty-five minutes we watched through the terminal windows, talking to the son, as a ground crew struggled to maneuver
the casket through the small opening in the plane. The
plane's departure was, of course, delayed. Finally Michael went out and spoke to the man in charge. Yes,
they had received the dimensions of the casket, but
they had forgotten that it had to be turned once it was
pushed through the opening, and that could not be
managed. Eventually they gave up. The casket was returned to a cool place for the night, and the next day it
was loaded aboard a plane with a roomy belly opening,
and began its trip to America.

The humdrum and the bizarre—in between lay those
responsibilities which for every American diplomat
abroad transcend the details, weighty or trivial, of his
office routine. He is a representative of his country, and
his private life may play a part for good or evil in the
conduct of America's foreign policy. Even to avoid
damaging his country's image is not the whole of his
private responsibility, because that is simply a nega-
tive approach to his career. There are a hundred little
ways in which he and his family may help. In his sub-
ordinate position, the entertainment of Pakistanis was
not among Michael's official duties Yet we wanted to
make many friends, not only as American representatives, but as human beings who would be enriched by
meeting as many different kinds of people as possible.

Thanks to some American friends we had already

made, we were introduced to a number of Pakistani
military men, and they were as lively a group as one
could meet anywhere. (It recalled many happy memories for us when several years later we again met a detachment of Pakistani troops who formed part of the
UN peace-keeping mission in the Congo.) Probably
the most memorable of these military men was General
I. Haji. Haji was not his real name, but one he had assumed after he had gone on *haj*, a pilgrimage to Mecca.
He was a fine-looking man, with iron-gray hair and a
gorgeous white mustache. His laugh was the deepest
and most infectious I have ever heard. His junior officers liked to call him "Lord Haw-Haw" (but not to his
face). It was a delight to entertain General Haji. The
evening seemed to revolve about him, and wherever one
was at a party one could hear, over the chatter and the
music, the great deep laugh of General Haji.

Several years later, when we were on home leave in
the United States, we saw him in Chicago. He had been
on another pilgrimage to Mecca. One of the privileges
which devolves on a man who has made such a pilgrimage is the right to "henna" his hair. You can't imagine my shock when I saw that his hair and his gorgeous mustache had been died a bright henna.

"Haji, what have you done?" I moaned

"What is the matter?" he asked, looking at me with
the utmost innocence.

"You know damn well what the matter is!" I said.

"You should go right home and wash that nasty stuff out of your hair!"

Thinking back on it now, I realize that I might have hurt his feelings by attacking him so suddenly, but I guess my instincts were good. The expression of innocence faded from General Haji's face and a look of mischievousness came over it, and suddenly the room was shaking as he broke out into that deep familiar laugh. He enjoyed my indignation almost as much as he enjoyed his own henna-ed hair.

There were other good Pakistani friends from those days, including H. S. Suharwardy, who had been the prime minister shortly before we arrived in Pakistan. He was always very gracious to us at his receptions and parties. Perhaps our best friends were the Mazaris. Sherbaz Mazari was a Baluch tribal chief who had settled in Karachi. His wife, Soriya, was in a kind of modified *purdah*. She could not see her brothers-in-law or her husband's cousins, but was free to go with me in the car or to the movies. She was one of the few Pakistani women I knew who had been educated. It was she who taught me the tricky art of winding a *sari*. If one has not mastered this art, the *sari* looks lumpy, with the tucks showing here and there. The secret was in the proper placement of two little tucks, which are not supposed to be visible.

The *saris* contributed to the extravagant settings of Pakistani dinner parties (a woman wears cotton *saris* during the day and silk *saris* in the evening). It was advisable, I found, to wear the *sari* just a bit short so that its folds didn't bunch at my feet. A *sari* is made up of six yards of material, and unravels easily. One evening I saw just how treacherous a *sari* can be for the unwary woman. After consuming five martinis, the wife of a Pakistani official tried to make her way upstairs to the ladies room. At the first step she tripped on her *sari*, which unraveled in a whirl and displayed more of its wearer than modesty prescribes.

Aside from Soriya Mazari, many of the other women we met in Karachi could not read or write, and were in some stricter stage of *purdah*. Although at the time the restrictions of *purdah* were slowly being relaxed among women of the upper classes, those in other classes of society continued to adhere to ancient customs; lower-class women did not venture into the streets without their heads and faces covered; even little girls had to wear a *burkah*, a full-length covering with a lacework opening to see through. If they lived at home, our servants wore their *burkahs* to our house, took them off while they worked and put them back on before leaving for home.

For a time we felt somewhat restricted in Karachi's social life because we were unable to entertain until the packing cases which held our extra dishes and table linens caught up with us. At last they arrived, and we fancied ourselves first-class citizens again. However, we still had to adjust in many ways to the customs of a new land. We learned, for instance, that it was risky to schedule a "sitdown" dinner. At the time we were in Karachi, the Pakistanis themselves were going through a sort of social revolution, with their women just coming into public life for the first time. Having planned a party, we would send out invitations to a number of couples, and they would be promptly accepted. Then, on the appointed evening, only the male Pakistanis would arrive for dinner, their wives unaccountably absent.

Nevertheless, one couldn't be certain whether the women would show up or not (some women did) and so most of our dinner parties were buffets. In that case, we didn't really care whether or not we knew in advance how many people would arrive. We simply prepared enough food to meet any eventuality, and saved what was left over. What was our chief dish? Stew. This was because in Karachi social life one could never be certain when pre-dinner cocktails would be set aside. If the assembled diplomats and businessmen had hold of an interesting topical subject, I found it extremely difficult to wheedle them in to the dinner table. It was best to have ready a dish that could be warmed over indefinitely. A stew was always "ready."

One precaution we took at first soon turned out to be unnecessary. We had understood that Moslems shunned liquor, as well as all forms of pork. We planned our first big party in Karachi soon after our dishes and linen arrived, and invited Americans, Pakistanis and what we called "third country" nationals, such as Filipinos. The roof of our home was an ideal place for a large party. We erected a tent there to protect our guests from the wind and brought in a phonograph so that we could dance. Before the guests arrived, we prepared Bloody Marys, assuming that the Moslems would not drink liquor and not wanting to have their drinks appear to be different from those of the other guests. We set glasses of plain tomato juice aside, sprinkling pepper on the glasses that had been spiked with vodka.

Early in the party, however, the head boy asked Michael to come aside. "Nobody drinks the tomato juice," he said. "They take only the drinks with the pepper on them."

Michael shrugged. "Okay," he said, "don't make any more without vodka."

Believe me, there were no complaints. Similarly, on the buffet we put dishes of ham, bacon and chicken. At the end of the evening we discoverd that the ham and bacon had disappeared, while the platters of chicken remained almost untouched.

Slowly we found ourselves accepted by the people of Karachi. There was, of course, a brief period of social "foot dragging." We discovered that one had to invite a Pakistani three or more times to one's home before receiving an invitation in return. But once the ice was broken, invitations to their homes came regularly. Occasionally, there were difficult moments. During one of our first evenings at a Pakistani home, a large silver tray was passed to the guests with the after-dinner coffee. The tray contained crushed betel nut, palm leaves, black tobacco and various seeds. The hostess began this stage of the evening by making a "pawn"—rolling up the crushed betel nut, spices and seeds in the leaves and offering them to her guests. Michael had wanted the opportunity to try the betel nut, a national delicacy. He accepted one and popped it into his mouth. I watched carefully before sampling mine. Suddenly his eyes bulged, his cheeks puffed out and he began to turn a very distinctive shade of red. Pushing back his chair, he excused himself as best he could and left the table. Somehow he was able to dispose of the bitter concoction before he choked on it, and eventually returned to the table, smiling but a trifle bleary-eyed. I left my betel nut untouched.

But mostly the dinners were pleasant affairs, with lavish tables and much too much food. A Pakistani host might serve a whole lamb to a small party of guests. And there was always chicken and rice, and those hot meat dishes which I came to like so well. For dessert there was usually a kind of custard, over which was spread a layer of extremely thin beaten silver. I found this covering tasteless, but it was easily digested and it added a sense of luxury to the meal.

But of all the outings in Karachi those that seemed to me the most fun occurred when someone rented one of the Bunder boats in the harbor and threw a party. The boats had wide lateen sails, and luxurious cushions were spread around the decks. Someone would bring a phonograph, and others would bring baskets of food and drinks. We ate and danced away the warm evenings while the crew propelled us, by sail and oar, around the harbor. The boats lacked one essential convenience. At intervals during the evening, the ladies would have to be rowed ashore to find rest rooms.

And through our Pakistani friends we attended many of the chief spectacles that took place during our stay in Karachi. There was the annual Independence Day Parade, during which we sat as guests of the generals. The streets were filled with color and noise, and as we watched from the reviewing stand, there passed dancing camels and kilted bagpipers, these last stepping grandly along in the British tradition. Afterward there was a lavish reception, where over the din we could hear repeatedly the deep laugh of our friend General Haji.

And there was the coronation of the Aga Khan. The most impressive sight I have ever seen was when this young man, destined to be the religious leader of the millions of his people, appeared in a plain white robe and accepted from his followers a jewel-encrusted robe, a jeweled sword and the Koran. He sat on a revolving jeweled throne, which turned him slowly and majestically to face each segment of the great circle of his people. Hidden in the intense heat of the pit beneath the throne were six men who kept the throne turning. From our seats we could see the commotion that occurred at regular intervals when one of the unfortunate men passed out. He was dragged from the pit, and another man was immediately dispatched to the inferno to replace him. It is not often that one is offered such a vivid picture of the misery that goes to sustain pomp and ceremony.

We found the Pakistanis a shy, gentle people, difficult to get to know sometimes because of their shyness, but immensely generous and outgoing. When we celebrated Christmas in Karachi, some of our Pakistani friends sent us presents. Michael and I received gifts bearing fantastic embroidery on them; Michael's were shoes, and mine leather bags. (Michael was a little startled at first with his shoes; the soles of embroidered Pakistani shoes were ordinarily fashioned from old rubber tires, but the workmen from whom our friends had ordered the shoes, in an effort to present Michael with "something special," had made him a pair with crepe soles!)

And suddenly one day we found ourselves in the middle of a serious national crisis. The government was overthrown. Later we read in American magazines that a "gory coup" had taken place under our noses, but I was unaware of any blood. Michael simply called from the Embassy one day to tell me to stay indoors. President Mirza was deposed and replaced by General Ayub Khan. A few shots were fired in front of the parliament building, and it was all over. Mirza and the Begum, his wife, were given one hour's notice to prepare to leave the capital. He was allowed to take four suitcases with him, and later those suitcases were rumored to have contained sufficient wealth for a man to live on in style for a hundred years. Mirza, however, later settled in modest circumstances in London.

But for our friends in the Pakistani army, the coup was an immense success. Most of them assumed positions of power in the new government. General Sheikh, whom we had entertained, became a minister in the cabinet; General Haji was appointed chief of the West Pakistan Industrial Development Corporation; other army friends were given key jobs in the various ministries and ordered to stamp out corruption and "instill the revolutionary spirit" into the flaccid bureaucracy.

It was our quietest crisis. Later we were to see governments shaken or toppled by greater violence.

6 ★
Fun and Games

I wish the Pakistani authorities published some sort of sporting encyclopedia. It would give me satisfaction to keep a copy of it on my bookshelf, and in the course of an evening when the conversation flagged, pull it down, and open to the heading "Fencing Champions of Pakistan." For there, under the entry for 1959, would be found the name "Michael P. E. Hoyt."

The listing would reflect one of the interesting and enjoyable pastimes we had while overseas. We drew upon our former experiences or hobbies and applied them in our new situation. While Michael was an undergraduate student at the University of Chicago, he took up fencing and became captain of the varsity team. During the intervening years of military service and married life he had let his foils rust, so to speak, but here in Karachi he found the opportunity to fence once more.

A Polish refugee named Tyminski, who served as a captain in the Pakistani navy, was also a fencing enthusiast. In his leisure moments Michael often went out to Captain Tyminski's training ship, which was anchored in the harbor. The two of them sharpened their technique while they taught the Pakistani navy boys some of the fundamentals. Finally a tournament was set up, and every local male who had an idea of how to hold his weapon or place his feet was induced to enter. In saber Michael proved master, and walked off with the championship.

It was such activities outside our normal routine that made up the raw material of so many later memories. We delved into projects which probably never would have occurred to us at home, or which never would have been possible. I was especially fortunate in this respect. Although I had a home to run, and three young children to bring up, I found myself in the enviable position of having time to do a great variety of things. There was little housework for me to be bothered with, aside from supervising the servants. Shopping, too, was not a time-consumer. Either the servants took care of the shopping in town, or I drove to the commissary founded by the families attached to the American Embassy. This was a co-operative venture, to which we each gave about $400 when we arrived in Karachi. The sustaining fund was returned to us when we left. The commissary ordered directly from the United States, but Europe often proved to be the cheapest and fastest source for getting good food.

I even found a man to sew for me. He was an itinerant worker who appeared periodically at our front door to ask if we had clothes, curtains or other items to be sewn. Once inside the house, he uncovered a funny old sewing machine, which looked like a toy and which he operated by turning a crank with his hand while grasping the fabric with his feet. He did very good work.

With these advantages I was free to take part in many of the projects initiated by the Embassy, or by the wives of American officials. I helped to distribute milk several times a week to the refugee children who had been forced to flee from India with their parents at the time of Independence. There was a great deal of poverty and misery among these people. It was my job to open the big five-pound cans of American powdered milk at the Embassy, and with a large electric beater, mix it with water in milk cans. The milk was then trucked to the distribution point, a refugee area. Besides the milling refugees, water buffaloes also used this place as a congregating point. I forced myself to ignore the odors, and dutifully stayed at my post, pouring the milk into beer cans we had saved to be used as cups and handing it out to the children.

A lot less painful, yet also helpful, was a project I worked on in connection with the annual British Bazaar. The British community in Karachi organized this bazaar to help support the local YWCA. It became very successful, and when the wives of American diplomats were offered a booth at the bazaar, we leaped at the opportunity to help. It was natural for us to want to offer something that was typically "American." What could be more appropriate, then, than an ice cream booth?

During my first year in Karachi, I served on the American committee for the bazaar with Betty Lewis, the wife of Geoffrey Lewis, the political counselor at the Embassy. We sold ice cream in paper cups, and did well. When bazaar time came around again the next year, I was asked to take over as chairman of the committee. I must do something a little different, I told myself. I wrote to a company in the United States which manufactured cones for ice cream dealers, and one of their executives wrote back to say that the company would let us have two thousand cones free of charge. His letter delighted me, but I still had to get the cones over to us. Pan American Airways came to my assistance here, offering to fly the cones to Karachi, also without charge.

The cones arrived promptly, less than a dozen of them having been broken in transit. I ordered the ice cream powder from the United States (which we paid for). At this point some officers in the United States Corps of Engineers, which had a construction project in Pakistan and a small organization in Karachi, stepped in to help. They made the ice cream and stored it in their huge walk-in freezer. After that, in view of the miserable ice cream which was available for sale in Karachi, our booth at the British Bazaar could not help but be a success. We made over $800 for the YWCA.

The wives of American Embassy officials held a meeting once a month at the Embassy residence. There we thought up projects that might be helpful, and assigned those of us who had free time to work on them. The meetings were usually confused and rambling, but we managed pretty well to keep to the order of business. I like to think that some good ideas came out.

One summer I was asked to teach arts and crafts at a nearby school. All of the children in one class were blind. I taught them basket-weaving. To another classroom of girls I taught sewing and embroidery. The most hectic of the classes was that in pottery. Every day a potter came in from the refugee camp, bringing his wheel and a pile of sand in a rickety donkey cart. He brought the sand in and dumped it on the classroom floor. To turn the wheel he used a piece of cane. It was quite a wild scene. At the end of the summer session the school authorities had to repaint the room.

As part of the program of the International Women's Club, to which I belonged in Karachi, we taught each other how to cook our national foods. This took us into Pakistani homes, where the women used to cook their "specialty" for us. I picked up a recipe for a Parsi dish made from fish baked in banana leaves. And, like Cinderella, I eventually emerged from the kitchen into the world of high fashion. Once the International Women's

Club staged a fashion show for Pakistani women, and I modeled Western clothes. On another occasion my friend Begum Mazari asked me to model Baluch costumes and jewelry at a charity event (because of *purdah*, she was not permitted to model them herself). Some newsreel service took pictures of the event, and before long I was receiving letters from friends in Indiana and Arizona who had seen me on the screen at their local movie houses.

There were many hours of relaxation, too. I've always loved to dance, and for a time I took lessons in Indian classical dancing from a Pakistani instructor. I wore slacks and went barefoot for my lessons; I would have preferred to wear shorts in that oppressive heat, but such a spectacle would certainly have outraged Pakistani sensibilities. American women acted strangely enough as it was!

But there were plenty of chances to cool off. With another American family we rented a beach house on the shores of the Arabian Sea, about ten miles from Karachi. The beach house, built of cement blocks, was a blessed haven for us on weekends when Michael could get away from his duties at the Embassy. The children loved it, not only for its sand and water, but for the camel rides on the beach, and the snake charmers who put on their scary shows before clusters of wide-eyed little vacationers.

Aside from our trips to the beach, there were few excursions for the entire family because, away from Karachi, it was almost impossible to secure food, water and milk free of the ubiquitous dysentery bugs. We felt that to drag the children over the Pakistani country-side, as fascinating for them as we knew such a trip to be, would be to court disaster. To compensate for this domestic policy of containment, we tried to keep things as lively as possible for the kids around home. There were occasional special entertainments, such as the Fourth of July party given at the Embassy every year by the American ambassador. It is traditional for the ambassador to pay for entertainment of Americans over-seas out of his own pocket. In the morning he would give a special reception for Pakistani officials and the diplomats from "third country" embassies. But the after-noons were given over to the American families, living there or just passing through the city. There was beer, soda pop, hot dogs and pony rides—which seemed as marvelous a treat to the children as the camel rides on the local beaches.

But the party which none of us will ever forget was the one we gave for Phelps at home on his third birthday. After supper the cook with great ceremony carried into the dining room a huge three-tiered cake, topped by icing and pasteboard decorations.

"Remove top, please," he said to me, grinning from ear to ear.

I lifted off the top of the cake and pulled back in sur-prise as three tiny birds flew out of the opening—one for each year of Phelps' young life! The children laughed and clapped and there was great excitement. The birds flew up to the ceiling and fluttered there and we rushed, very nearly too late, to turn off the *punkah*, the big slow-moving overhead fan, to keep the birds from becoming entangled in it. It was a beautiful moment, and we'll always be grateful to that smiling Pakistani cook who knew how to delight a three-year-old boy.

7 ★
A Sad Affair

There are those travelers (we can all think of a few of them among our friends) who fly to some distant foreign city, are whisked from the airport to a Hilton hotel or its counterpart, look out over the city for a while from the broad-windowed cocktail lounge, then return to America to talk about the "charming" city they have visited. They might just as well have stayed in Chicago.

To know a city and to think of it with affection, one has to have lived with it "for better or worse." The "worse" in Karachi was very, very bad. For each delight there was often an uneasy moment. Water was a problem for us from the very beginning. Because there was very little of it trickling through the pipes of the overextended water system into our section of the city, the American Embassy provided us with water through a local dealer. It was brought to our house in trucks (nearly a thousand gallons a day) and poured into a water tank behind the house. Nevertheless, this water was as impure as any other that could be found around the city. We boiled all we drank (the Pakistanis seemed to be amused at the way Americans always boiled their water, and there was a rumor in the city that we even boiled the water we poured into the radiators of our automobiles). With three small children, however, we couldn't be too careful. Our kids had a habit of drinking their bath water, so we would add Detal (a British-manufactured version of Lysol) to it, hoping it would somewhat mitigate the harmful effects.

During an acute water shortage which hit the city while we were there, even our deliveries almost stopped and the five of us had to bathe in the same water. I suffered from amoebic dysentery four different times. Once I was really miserable, and I felt so weak that I could hardly crawl out of bed during the day. The doctor specified that I bring stool samples to him "hot off the griddle." I accomplished that by freezing them, and then carrying them around to him when I felt able to move. After analyzing them in the laboratory, he came out shaking his head.

"Young lady," he said mournfully, "you should be dead."

I took an arsenic cure for my troubles, and at times the cure seemed worse than the disease.

Despite our precautions with the children, Phelps

came down with what we first thought to be "Karachi tummy," or a violent case of diarrhea. The poor little fellow was miserable. I took him to the Seventh Day Adventist Hospital in Karachi (we had no doctor attached to the Embassy at that time). The doctor gave me some powders to feed him, but they didn't help. Next I took him to Holy Family Hospital. The Mother Superior, after looking Phelps over, came back into the room with an armful of material; she had some dried apple grated into a tin, some white powders which she had done up in little papers, and a repulsive-looking black liquid concoction.

"Give these to him," she said to me.

"What's wrong with him?" I asked.

"I don't know what's wrong with him," the Mother Superior said. "But something's wrong, so he'd better take this."

I took the mess home and disposed of it quickly. Then I made arrangements for Phelps to see the World Health doctor. This doctor was supposed to be in Karachi only to set up a pediatric clinic at the public hospital, not to practice medicine. He agreed, however, to look at Phelps in his spare time. I drove Phelps, who was sicker than ever, to the public hospital. There were people camped out all over the stairs. We had to crawl over them to get to the doctor's office on the second floor. These people, who were relatives of patients, assembled there when any member of their family was ill. They laid out blankets and brought along pots in which they cooked their food over fires in the yard. It seems that formerly these people had infested the pediatric ward, sleeping under the beds of the child patients, until the newly arrived World Health doctor threw them out. The children had had absolutely no chance to rest or to recover under those unsettled conditions.

Yet when I reached the pediatric clinic on the second floor I was impressed by its cleanliness, and told the doctor so.

"Come look at this," he said, and beckoned to me to follow him. He led me to a sink with a single water tap. "We finally have running water in here," he said proudly. "It's only cold water, but it's the first we've had."

He examined Phelps, and then broke the news to me. The poor little fellow was suffering from paratyphoid fever. The preventative shots he had been given before leaving the United States had not covered a special type of the germ found in Karachi. Perhaps he had taken a forbidden sip of the bath water. In any case, Phelps quickly responded to treatment, and soon he was as good as new again.

It was my experience, as you will see later, that many Pakistanis, even in an emergency, harbored a reluctance which amounted almost to dread when they were asked to donate their blood. At the Embassy all of us had been asked, against an emergency, to have our blood typed and recorded. One Saturday morning, as Michael and I were leaving for the beach with the children, the phone rang. It was the Embassy calling. A Pakistani woman, gravely ill in Holy Family Hospital, needed blood. Since mine was on record as being the right type, would I go?

I said of course I would, and rushed to the hospital. There the nuns asked me to lie on a bed. The blood was siphoned from my arm into a tube, which funneled it into a jar lying on the floor beside the bed. When the jar had been filled one of the nuns rushed it upstairs, turned it upside down and siphoned the blood into the woman's veins.

Whatever happened to the unfortunate woman, I do not know. But following an incident that occurred sometime later in the United States, I had some uneasy moments. Scot hemorrhaged during a tonsilectomy, and the doctors asked for my blood type in case a transfusion became necessary. I consulted a card I had kept with me since those days in Karachi, and gave them the type noted on it. The doctors analyzed my blood to confirm this, then told me that a mistake had been made when they had typed it in Karachi!

But no uncertainties remain to dim the memory of the genuine tragedy which later was played out around us in Karachi. The cook's wife, a thin little young thing who had never looked very well to me, became pregnant. I suggested to the couple that as a Christmas present I send the woman to the hospital to have her baby at my expense. They were pleased by my offer.

I made arrangements with the hospital, and drove the

woman there for her first checkup. She wasn't feeling well, she told me in the car on the way. No wonder! After examining her, the doctor came out and told me that she was nearly dead from anemia; the woman needed two pints of whole blood immediately. If we bought the blood from the hospital, the cost would be $35 a pint. If it was donated, there would be no charge.

According to my Embassy records, my blood wouldn't do. I drove home and rounded up her husband and the other servants and brought them back to the hospital with me. The doctor reported that the husband and the night watchman had the correct type of blood for the transfusion. He asked the pair to go with him. The watchman reluctantly followed, but the woman's husband refused to budge.

"Go in with the doctor," I told him.

He shook his head, and his eyes were positively jumping with fright. He wouldn't go.

"You're crazy," I shouted at him. "You get the hell in there and *give!*

No, he was afraid. I told him to go. No, he was afraid. Why? I asked him. Well, his friend had told him that a person had only two pints of blood in his body, and that if he lost that quantity he could never make it up and he would die. I assured him that he had plenty to spare, and pushed him after the doctor.

The transfusions were successful and the woman returned home. I continued to take her to the hospital for periodic checkups. Her time came about two o'clock one morning, and Michael and I got out of bed and rushed her to the hospital. The baby, a little girl, was born weighing only two pounds and four ounces. The people at the hospital gave the little thing excellent care and nursed it along. For a while we hung on every breath it took. The baby remained in the hospital until it weighed five pounds, when she was released to her parents. I looked out the window one morning and saw the cook and his wife bringing her home. It was a satisfying triumph over long odds.

Three days later the baby choked to death. Michael and I were awakened about five in the morning by a chilling wail and the sound of someone pounding on our door. Michael leaped out of bed and opened the door. The mother stood there, screaming and trembling.

"The baby!" she kept screaming. "The baby!"

We rushed with her to the servants' quarters, and found the baby dead in her crib. Apparently the mother had given her a two o'clock feeding—and propped the bottle! Then, leaving the weak little creature, she had gone to bed and not returned until dawn.

I was crushed by the senselessness of it. Michael and I gave the couple twenty rupees (about four dollars) to pay for the funeral, which was set for the same day and was attended only by men, which is the Moslem custom. But the woman helped her husband wrap the body in a blanket, and then the bundle was wrapped again in a straw mat. Michael and I watched the two of them walk down the road together, the little bundle under the man's arm, toward the mosque.

Soon life was going on again as usual. The family returned from the funeral and washed all their clothes and their bodies, scrubbed their rooms and moved outside to live there for three days. Since they could not light a fire during their period of mourning, their friends brought them food every day. And then the mourning was over and they were back at work.

8 ★
The Northwest Frontier

Michael must have thought we had gone out of our minds. Most of the other men thought so, too. Who would want to make such a trip, when the gains were so little and the effort so great?

It all began when two of the economic officers at the Embassy, Tom Robinson and Dennis Kux, planned a trip to Hyderabad on business. This city, which is not to be confused with the larger one in central India, lies about a hundred miles northwest of Karachi, and its chief distinction seems to be that it succeeded Karachi as the provincial capital after Independence. Doris Robinson had a sudden desire to accompany her husband and asked Ethel Schiff and me to go along with her. It became something of an adventure for us. We would go there by car and return by train.

Our husbands raised their eyebrows, but offered no

objections to the plan. We were warned, however, not to take a large amount of money with us in the event we were robbed. This warning wasn't very encouraging, but we stuck to our plan. It turned out to be one of those experiences that you are glad to have had, but that you would not undertake again. The drive up was uneventful except for a stop at a lovely mosque, one of the few that women could enter. We skirted the edge of the great Sind desert, through a dusty sun-baked land. After looking around Hyderabad, which looked like a crossroad leading to some place else, we bought first-class tickets and boarded the Karachi train. The "first class" seats consisted of hard boards, and the coach itself was hot and dusty. The train was unbelievably slow. We stopped at every crossroad, where vendors came aboard and walked through the coaches, selling tea, soda pop, round unleavened bread and very tough roasted corn. We encountered no cutpurses. After an all-day trip we arrived at Karachi, tired and grimy but exhilarated by our quiet adventure.

The climate, which I had thought would make us lethargic, in fact exerted the opposite effect. And although the days in Karachi were very hot and humid, usually there was some breeze and the nights were comfortably cool. It was the city's humidity or its dust which depressed us, and at those times we craved the coolness and greenness of northern mountains. Michael, in fact, had hoped for a time to be transferred to the Consulate in Peshawar, only ten miles from the Khyber Pass on the Northwest Frontier. The lure of the mountains and their spectacular surroundings, besides the added responsibilities that would be his in a smaller post, had turned his thoughts in that direction, but the transfer never became a reality.

The mountains themselves, partly because of friendships we had made since our arrival in Karachi, became a glorious reality. Michael and I wanted to see as much as possible while we were stationed in Karachi, and in our two years there we eventually covered a good deal of the great subcontinent. One of our most enjoyable trips was made in the company of a group of diplomats and their wives. Rawalpindi, now the capital of Pakistan, was our headquarters for the excursion. It was then that we finally saw the green mountains we had craved. Our group, which included several Indians and a Russian diplomat, flew to Rawalpindi from Karachi in a Pakistani air force plane. The next day we drove into the mountains to Murree. The hills reminded me so much of Colorado, with its tall evergreens and oceans of wild flowers. We walked past little houses built into the hillsides, and sat on the grass—I had forgotten how green grass could be!—and ate oranges.

And on the following day we drove to Kakul, which is Pakistan's West Point, for the graduation ceremonies. The day was cold and rainy and we did not have rain gear with us, and the car broke down three times on the way. But nobody cared. We were in a holiday mood and every mishap was only an incident to laugh over. I

remember the ceremony itself as "the fainting parade."
Several Pakistani soldiers collapsed in the ranks, probably from the tension. Afterward we went to the officers'
mess for lunch and a reception, at which the Pakistani
prime minister presided. I have never seen so many generals, resplendent in their uniforms with bright red
shoulder boards, in one room. The weather had cleared
by this time and after a five-course luncheon we
walked out onto the lawn for coffee. We had a marvelous time. The diplomatic group was as frisky as a bunch
of kids, and the Pakistani generals let down their mono-
cles and joined in the fun. The Russian appeared a bit
stiff, and some of the other Americans were ill at ease
and reluctant to unbend.

On the way back to Rawalpindi we noticed that the
Indians were riding together in the same car with the
Russian diplomat.

"Something's up," Michael whispered, nudging me.

Sure enough, as we came to a road that led to an ordi-
nance plant, their car abruptly turned off. Almost immediately a Pakistani major roared around us in his
car, giving chase. There was to be no spy stuff on this
holiday. The major herded the errant car back into line
and the incident was forgotten. When we got back to
Rawalpindi there was a dance at the home of one of the
generals. I danced with everybody, including the Russian, who stepped all over my feet but enjoyed himself
immensely.

There was a trip to India later on to see the great historic sites. We flew to Delhi, where we toured forts and mosques and ruins—and then went shopping. From there we flew to Agra and the Taj Mahal. There are some objects or views which have been so frequently written about, that when at last you come to see them you feel a numbing letdown, no matter how great the effort to work up the proper emotional and aesthetic responses. It is marvelous, you agree, it is well worth seeing, yet somehow—isn't there more? But there are two sites that you have read about and heard about for years and nevertheless when you come to see them for the first time you are completely overwhelmed. Even the most artful descriptions, you find, have conveyed no sense of their grandeur. One of these is the Grand Canyon, and the other is the Taj Mahal.

We luxuriated in this building, as a child might roll in tall grass on a summer day. We wandered among screens of hand-carved marble, and descended to the tombs below, where one's echo lingers for a quarter of a minute. We each took a wishing thread, in exchange for a donation, and were assured by the attendant that their powers were so tangible that men had used them to wish their enemies into an early death. My wish was more bland; in fact, I have forgotten it. Outside again, we stared up at those minarets from which visitors were barred because unhappy lovers had so often taken advantage of their great height to put a prompt end to their misery. The minarets, which were built so that they lean slightly away from the main structure itself in

order that they might not damage it if they ever toppled, were undergoing at this time some extensive re-
construction. Michael found fragments of marble on the
ground nearby, and came away with a souvenir.

But probably the most exciting of all the trips we took
in Pakistan was to the northwestern frontier areas near
Afghanistan and Russia. Our friend in the Pakistani
army, Brigadier General Mohammed Hayat, had arranged the trip for us. With Walter and Joyce Cox, another American couple at the Embassy, Michael and I
toured an extensive area not normally open to foreigners.

We drove all the way in a Mercedes, with clothes and
food stuffed into three foot lockers tied on the roof. We
started from Karachi, going up the Indus to Sukkur and
branching north to Quetta, the southern gateway to the
Northwest Frontier. We paralleled the Afgan border to
Fort Sandeman, entering wild tribal lands, and headed
north to Peshawar and the Khyber Pass. We saw Russia from the Hindu Kush kingdom of Swat, and then took
the back way to Murree through the region of Kashmir
controlled by Pakistan. Then we drove straight south
from Lahore across the Punjab and followed the Indus
once again to Karachi.

During most of the trip we were the guests of the
army, not only for our comfort but also for our safety.
The British had never succeeded in pacifying the Northwest Frontier. The tribal people in the hills have re-
tained their fierce and independent spirit for centuries,

and the establishment of Pakistan after World War II has changed little for them.

We drove into these frontier hills escorted by armed trucks riding ahead of us and behind. Once, when the lead truck broke down, soldiers poured from both trucks, according to standard orders, and deployed out on all sides, blending into the rocks, rifles ready, to defend our party in case of an attack from the surrounding hills. In some of the places we visited—Quetta, Peshawar, Saidu Sharif (which is the capital of Swat) and Rawalpindi—we stayed in hotels like other tourists. In other places—Fort Sandeman, Jondola and Bannu—we stayed in army quarters. I'll never forget our arrival at one remote fort near the Afghan border. I felt as if I were part of a 1930 movie about colonial India as we rode into the fort with our heavily armed escort and found tea waiting for us, served on tables covered with rough white cloths.

A contrasting spectacle was that at Rojan, a village belonging to our friend Mazari's tribe, the Baluchs. We were quartered in the Audience Hall, where the grandfather of the present tribal chief, Sherbaz Khan Mazari's brother, had once held court. The village lay on a river bank in starkly barren country. The hall, however, was sumptuous: there were hand-carved doors inlaid with mother-of-pearl, high mirrored ceilings, and Persian carpets into which we sank almost to our knees.

The day after our arrival at Rojan we went into the hills for a deer shoot. The hill people we saw there looked the part of warriors, for they maintained the old traditions of the Baluch tribe; their kinsmen who have moved to the towns showed the softening influences of civilization. We rode in jeeps across the rocky plains, our bones vibrating under the jarring pace. Once we became bogged down in a sandy place, and it took a while for the jeeps to work themselves free. At another point even the tribesmen weren't sure where we were. We wandered aimlessly for a little while, and finally spied in the distance the fort where we were to have lunch. We had not seen any deer, but I was happy to be out of the wilderness.

The "lunch" proved to be a feast. The tribesmen served us a whole goat, six chickens, five curries, two great platters of rice, two bowls of sweet rice, fruits, nuts and coffee. Seven of us did our best to consume it all.

Afterward the tribal leaders came to pay their respects to us. They were the most handsome men I have ever seen. They never shaved or cut their hair, and had masses of black hair sticking out from under their white turbans. A shooting contest was arranged for our entertainment. Much to the amazement of the tribal people, who keep their wives at home, I joined in, having done some shooting during my college years. There was a great uproar when, after the tribesmen had shot and missed at a pot they had set up some two hundred yards away, I knocked it over with my first shot!

"When you go home you should give your wife your

rifle," the tribal chief told the embarrassed tribesmen, "and you should put on her *burkah*."

Since a Baluch would never be seen without his rifle, this was a great insult to them and I felt a little apprehensive. But apparently the chief can indulge in this sort of teasing, and nothing further was said about the matter.

A woman returns from such trips with more than delightful memories. Michael had his souvenir of the Taj Mahal in the form of a discarded fragment of marble. I am afraid that my souvenirs were gathered at greater cost.

In my two years in Karachi I had wandered through the bazaars, shopping for bargains for myself and my relatives in America. I was forever buying brass and copper bowls, native sandals, shoes covered with silverwork, and native costumes. But my prize from Karachi was a genuine camel chest that I had bought in the bazaar for one hundred rupees, or about twenty dollars. The chest is made of solid teakwood, with brass fixtures, and comes apart into two equal parts. I like to think this chest crossed the deserts, carried by a stately camel in some legendary caravan. For an additional hundred rupees I was able to have the chest redone, taken down to the natural wood, and oil rubbed into it for a satin finish.

My trips out of Karachi, through the remainder of Pakistan and into India, included more frenzied shopping. In Rawalpindi, I bought enormous baskets used to carry grain. In Taxila, I found a bowl—carved from stone and gaily painted—for grinding spices. In India, I bought a white cashmere stole (the word cashmere, of course, comes from Kashmir, that beautiful land which remains a bone of bitter contention between Pakistan and India), and bolts of silk and madras cotton, all of which I shipped back to the United States.

And now, as Michael's assignment in Karachi neared its close, I began to look forward to our trip home—by way of Hong Kong and the Pacific Ocean. This route was attractive to me because it would complete our trip around the world. I also wanted to see the shops of Hong Kong after two years in Karachi and the limited opportunities to purchase standard items I would need for our next post.

9.★

A Change of Scene

It was the crazy stuffed goat that I recall best from our
period of leave-taking—and I believe it should stand as
a symbol of all such leave-takings. This was a feverish
period. Packing up and saying good-bye are both full-
time procedures, and combining the two produces a
special kind of uproar. The goods we had accumulated
during our two years in Karachi had to be stuffed into
trunks and crates, and the excess disposed of. Looking
up from a disordered trunk, we would suddenly realize
that we were due at another in the round of farewell
parties, a gesture so generous on the part of our friends
that we couldn't help but feel some embarrassment as
one farewell followed another.

Only after the last dish had been wrapped and crated
and the last cotton dress folded into a trunk did the goat
enter our lives. There was to be one "positively-the-end"

party on the night before our departure. As the high point of the evening, our friends gathered around and presented us with our "farewell" gift. What emerged from the wrappings was the most enormous and insipid-looking life-sized stuffed goat you ever saw! And it epitomized for us so many other farewell gifts that people give each other on such occasions: it was both useless and too bulky to carry.

But I have moved much too fast through the preceding days. The parties were bright oases in an otherwise uninterrupted frenzy of preparations. They were respites when we could sit back and indulge ourselves in the recollection of friends we had made and sights we had seen. Tempering our regret at the moment of taking leave of our old friends was the excitement that such a step implied. Ahead of us lay a vacation with friends and relatives in the United States, and beyond that the challenge of a new post in still another foreign land. But at the end of every party lay the task of packing up, an overwhelming job for a family of five which is equipped to live and entertain in a foreign city.

We were able to jettison part of our belongings. We sold the "220" appliances to families which had just arrived. We gave all our medicines, so difficult to come by in Karachi, to our friends. Although we were returning to the United States for home leave, we had the advantage of knowing where we would go from there. Michael's orders called for three months of leave and conferences in the States; he was then to report to Casablanca, Morocco, to take up his new duties as economic officer and vice-consul. We would, therefore, ship most of our household belongings directly to Casablanca.

With the help of servants and handymen, we began the packing. The most onerous job was handling the dishes and china. Breakage (I am very good in this department) cut down on the supply of glasses and dishes, yet there were stacks of them remaining. I remember two dozen water goblets, four dozen wineglasses, eighteen or twenty brandy glasses (mostly unmatched) and about six dozen highball glasses (most of which had been sent us by the liquor companies in England from whom we and the other American families in Karachi ordered whiskey by the case).

During the respites from packing we shopped for a few last-minute articles we would need for the trip home. Phelps, for instance, badly needed shoes. I took him to the Karachi shop of a British firm which made cheap shoes in all conceivable colors.

"What kind of shoes would you like, Phelps?" I asked him.

"Orange."

"I said what kind of shoes would you like?"

"Orange."

Orange it had to be, and Phelps left for the United States in the brightest pair you can imagine. It reflected his mood, I suppose. All the children had been looking forward to going "home" for several months now, and as we boarded the big BOAC Comet in Karachi, they were terribly excited at our first jet trip.

There were stops in Delhi, Bombay, Bangkok, and suddenly we were in Hong Kong. Having sold our Chevrolet in Karachi, I was fortified by the kind of cash I do not ordinarily have. Most of it disappeared quickly. A friend who had recently returned to Karachi from Hong Kong had given me a list of stores where we could have suits, shoes and other articles made to order. Michael and I set off on a shopping spree. Our orders were quickly filled. For instance, we were able to pick up our shoes the day after we had been fitted for them. We ordered porch furniture, table linens, kitchen chairs and luggage. We even visited the old section of the city, where one can buy dishes absurdly cheap; good cups and saucers were a nickel apiece. Most of what we bought we ordered to be packed and shipped to our new address in Casablanca. Gifts—ivory elephants, linens, silk pajamas—for our friends we shipped directly to the United States. I even found time to visit the local Elizabeth Arden's and have my hair dressed.

Meanwhile, the children were in good hands. Friends who lived in Hong Kong sent the mother of their *ahyma*, or nanny, to our hotel. She was a lovely old woman, whom the kids immediately took an interest in. She shepherded them all over the city, took them for rides in rickshaws, and even arranged for them to ride the ferry across to Kowloon on the Chinese mainland, where they were able to buy *real* ice cream. In the evenings we returned from shopping and sightseeing to take the kids to dinner. Their desires were very definite. They insisted on hamburgers and hot dogs at Gingle's, while Phelps ordered an extra dish of eggs (the chickens in Pakistan were reported to be suffering from some kind of tuberculosis while we were there, and eggs were a very rare treat for us indeed). Meanwhile, the old Chinese woman insisted on staying at the hotel to wash the children's clothes by hand, claiming that the infinitely small charge for laundry at the hotel was "too much." We paid her one dollar a day.

From Hong Kong we flew to Tokyo, intending to remain there for a few days, then perhaps see some other parts of Japan. But Phelps became ill and we decided to move on. We flew to Honolulu and took him to the hospital there for an examination. The doctor looked him over, and much to our relief, ascribed his illness to "exhaustion." The little fellow had just done and seen too much.

"Get him back to the States and let him rest," the doctor told me. He gave him a shot of phenobarbital and sent him on his way. When we arrived in San Francisco and the plane taxied to a stop, Phelps, dazzling in his orange shoes, was the first one off the plane.

Michael had accumulated almost two months of home and regular leave. As a junior Foreign Service officer, he was entitled to fifteen days' leave every day, in addition to one and a half days for each month of overseas duty. We took the children to Snowflake, Arizona, where my sister was staying that summer. Snow-flake! Even the name carried the promise of a delightful contrast to Karachi's heat and humidity. When we had left for Karachi, Phelps and Scot had been too young to gather any memories of the United States. Now, in Arizona's cool mountains, the two younger children "discovered" America.

Television was a revelation. So were many of the other things that most American kids take for granted —Cokes and ice cream which tasted as they were supposed to, water that could be drunk right out of the faucets, hamburgers that didn't taste like water buffalo. The children fished in mountain streams, and went to the rodeo, an exotic excursion for my three little "Asiatics." Fresh milk was another novelty, although I am afraid their Karachi diet of powdered milk had forever prejudiced them against that beverage in any form whatsoever. Perhaps the most cherished aspect of America for the children was the freedom to run about on their own without having to be tended by an older person or being contained in a compound. America's "freedom" came to have a very special meaning for them.

Reunion with our relatives was a treat for me, but there were some pressing matters to be taken care of before I could relax completely. We had learned that we would not be able to find a suitable furnished house in our new post. We ordered our furniture to be taken out of the warehouse in Washington and shipped to Casablanca. Through export houses in New York we were able to order a new deep freeze, a refrigerator, a stove and a washing machine. These, too, were shipped immediately, to make certain that they arrived before we did. Thus we had four different heavy shipments converging on our new home: furniture from Washington, Karachi and Hong Kong, and appliances from New York. One of the necessities of establishing a home overseas is that heavy articles be shipped two or three months in advance, even to seaports such as Karachi and Casablanca. More time must be allowed for inland cities.

While Michael flew to Washington to consult with State Department officials before taking on his new assignment, I finished the shopping in Arizona. This, for the most part, was accomplished in clothing stores. Three growing children had to be outfitted again for a subtropical climate. Though there were purchases to make for Michael and me, they were not as essential. One's old clothes are always "new" to the next post.

As the time came to begin another round of farewells, the allure of television and milk shakes faded for the children and they looked forward to our new life as anxiously as we did. This time getting there was *really* half the fun. We sailed from New York on the liner *Independence,* seven days to Casablanca.

The ship presented a wonderful rest for me, and a wonderful new world for the children to explore. Even the disappearance of Phelps' bag, with nearly all his traveling clothes, from the luggage cart on the New

York pier failed to upset us. We carried a great deal of luggage, fourteen pieces, including two foot lockers, on that voyage. (We had given up an old steamer trunk because we never know when we might have to fly, and a steamer trunk is strange and puzzling to everybody concerned at an airport.) Anyway, we did not miss Phelps' bag until we were at sea. He survived very well, in a pair of old pants and a white shirt that said "SS IN-DEPENDENCE" in big block letters across the front. Fortunately, I had packed his best white shirt in my own bag. Phelps wore it to dinner every night, and then I washed it out and hung it up to dry for use the next night. Phelps was not a very tidy eater in those days.

10 ★
On the Rim of Africa

Casablanca! It is a name that tempts one to weave all sorts of romantic notions about it. The name evokes scenes of international intrigue, peopled by world leaders like Roosevelt and Churchill, or shady characters who act and talk like Bogart. Smugglers, veiled ladies, swarthy detectives. From the promenade deck of the *Independence* we looked across the water to a gleaming white city set in the hilly North Africa coastline. Here the vague romantic notions were to be dissolved in the reality of our own lives. Michael was to take on the responsibility and hard work he had asked for. The children and I, establishing ourselves again in a strange city, would confront another face of the world, yet try to retain our entity as an American family. And here our fourth child would come into the world, not without a struggle. We left the ship and set foot for the first time on the soil of Africa.

For Michael, who had studied French and who wanted to specialize in African affairs, this colorful port in the former French protectorate of Morocco was an ideal introduction to the continent. His duties at the American Consulate were to be quite varied. As economic officer and vice-consul, he would be involved with almost every phase of Consulate business, handling economic and commercial duties, as well as relieving others on some of the consular and administrative work. Though Casablanca is not the capital city of the kingdom (Rabat is the capital), it is one of Africa's most important seaports. Most of the country's imports and exports are funneled through this city.

Our first home in Casablanca was the Anfa Hotel, where Roosevelt and Churchill had met in 1943 before issuing the announcement that World War II could end only with Germany's unconditional surrender. By the time we arrived, many of its luxurious suites and rooms had been converted into apartments, its huge closets made over into kitchens, and children played where world figures and their aides and bodyguards had once hustled. We remained there for six weeks. The Consulate did not provide us with housing as the Embassy had done in Karachi, and house-hunting was arduous in this city where housing was scarce. Those were difficult weeks, for the Hoyts are not apartment dwellers.

At last we found a house. The section was slightly

down-at-heel, for many of the more well-to-do people had moved out near the ocean, but it was a large and charming house within walking distance of the Consulate. This was a saving for us, because it meant that we could make do with one car. We paid $150 a month for the house, which was exactly the amount allowed us by the government for housing overseas.

The house sat in a little walled garden with palm trees all around it. The rooms had high ceilings, and French doors, rather than windows, gave from the living room onto the garden. The bathrooms, in our sense, were compartmentalized—toilets in one room, tubs and basins in another. Because of the local dampness and mildew there were no closets, and one of my first projects was to order metal poles from Sears, Roebuck. From these we fashioned racks on which to hang our clothes.

The local prevalence of bugs also influenced the furnishings. Rugs, in which bugs are apparently snug, were taboo. Instead, we lived on bare terrazzo floors, an advantage in one way because they could be so easily hosed down every morning. We learned what any cop on the beat could have told us, however; to pound across stone floors all day and go up and down the unyielding stairs can be very uncomfortable. We insisted the children keep their shoes on indoors to prevent them from breaking down their arches on the terrazzo.

Fortunately, there had been plenty of time for our furniture and appliances to arrive before we moved in.

Now, the house settled, I was able to go on to other matters. Chief among these was registering the children in school. Casablanca had a large European population, the French, of course, being in the majority. Many of the Moroccans, too, spoke French. Since Michael already had a solid background in the language and I began lessons almost immediately, it seemed a good idea to place the children in a French school. The school we selected for them accepted children from the age of three, so we sent all of them. They were placed in kindergarten until they had learned enough French to be able to get along on their proper level. Reed, who was then nine, took arithmetic on his own grade level but returned to kindergarten for the rest of his work. The kids picked up the language quickly and were soon moved into the proper classes, but it was about six months before they could understand and speak enough French to compete with their classmates.

On the whole, the children enjoyed the experience. Reed, it is true, complained that the school served wine mixed with water for lunch, and he did not like it. The school granted him permission to drink his water straight. But though they survived, I think now that we made a mistake. Unless one plans eventually to send a child on to a European university, the child is undoubtedly handicapped in a "foreign language" school because he misses those vital early years when he learns to get along in his own language. Later, when we had the children in school in Illinois, Scot's teacher there asked

me to come in and talk over her problems. She told me
that while Scot was on grade level in arithmetic, she
couldn't say her ABC's or count in English, as all the
other children could.

Another drawback for the children, I thought, was
the French school's insistence on competition. A sense
of competition among the students was nurtured to the
point of obsession. There was little attempt to teach the
children to get along with each other, no recess periods
or games when the children could learn that give-
and-take which is so important later on in life. Great
emphasis was placed on winning medals in class. So intense was this competition that even some time afterward when we took the children to Italy on a vacation
and paid a visit to the Vatican, they were instantly
attracted to the medals displayed in the glass cases
along the walls.

"Look!" I heard them call excitedly to one another.
"Here's one just like the medal they gave us for arithmetic!"

During our last year in Casablanca we transferred
Reed to the school operated by the United States Government at the Air Force base in nearby Nouasseur.

The children felt quite at ease in Casablanca. We
lived in an area where there were other families who
had children, and after school Reed, Phelps and Scot
found a number of playmates among the Swiss and
Italian boys and girls whose fathers were diplomats.
Nearby there was a small USO for American service-

men stationed in Morocco, and there the children could
buy American ice cream, candy bars and magazines.

I, too, was delighted by the shopping that I found in
the nearby local markets. This was a truly sensuous experience, too often denied us now in this world of
cellophane-wrapped foods picked off the shelves in antiseptic supermarkets. Of all the good things in Casablanca, I would have to put the bread at the top of the
list. There was a baker just around the corner from us.
At some time during the morning we would begin to
smell the French bread, that bread which is incomparable. At eleven o'clock it would be ready. I would dash
around the corner and buy several yard-long flutes, or
loaves. Before I got back to the house I would have consumed half a loaf. This warm bread, fresh every morning, spoiled the children (as did the homemade bread
in Karachi) for the tasteless stuff they found back in the
United States. They loved to make sandwiches of it, or
just eat it as they would eat cake.

In Morocco, as in most of the Mediterranean countries
(while Casablanca is on the Atlantic Ocean, part of the
country borders the Mediterranean Sea), the people do
their shopping every day. I suppose this habit is necessary in a warm country that is largely without refrigera-
tors. Yet it has its nonutilitarian delights, too. One's
fruits and vegetables are always fresh. Only a few
blocks from us were the vegetable markets, a clean,
fresh-smelling region where the vegetables, shining

green, red and yellow, were piled invitingly in the covered stalls. I always wanted to buy everything I laid
my eyes on.

In these markets one could also find all sizes and
shapes of French cheeses, real cheeses and not the proc-
essed kind that smells no more pungently than store
margarine. There were small meat markets nearby, too,
but the variety was limited and we often went downtown to the larger markets to buy our meat. Pork, for
instance, was not stocked by the smaller shops because
of the Moslem dietary prohibitions on it, and so one
had to order it in advance. The alternative was to
search out downtown one of the shops which special-
ized in pork. (Here, as in France, there were separate
shops also where horse meat was sold, identified by the
big shiny gold horse's head mounted on a red sign.)

But our favorite dishes in Casablanca contained
either lamb or fish. Both were always fresh, and gave
to the meal a sense that we were taking part in a feast.
On Sunday mornings we would drive downtown to the
big markets and wait for the lobsters to come in. After
selecting our lobsters, we would take them home and
cook them, and eat them later on the terrace with white
wine and French bread. I still dream about those Sunday meals.

Wine truly was cheaper than water in Casablanca.
We carried our empty wine bottles to the big department store where they sold good wine drawn from big
tanks. You simply held your empty bottle under the

spigot until it was filled, at a cost of only a few cents a liter. For a treat, we bought a wonderful rosé, bottled in Morocco, which Michael still thinks of as his favorite wine. But every meal there was special! For desserts there were fresh fruits from the market, eaten with the French cheese, and rich pastries from the nearby *pâtisserie*. The table itself was always piled with bouquets, as were most of our rooms, because the markets overflowed with fresh flowers—daisies and glads and corn flowers—which cost next to nothing.

There was another side to the coin, of course. Fresh milk was not available here, either, and the kids tried their best to swallow the powdered milk. Cokes, outside of the American commissary and the USO, were blended for the Moroccan market, which demanded that they be, according to our taste, excessively sweet. And clothing in Casablanca was very expensive. One of the few items I bought for myself there was a bikini, and that wasn't easy. I just couldn't get one to fit me. Then a friend tipped me off: in buying a bikini one chooses a top of this size, and a bottom of that size. As long as you match up the material in both pieces, the "suit" seems to come out just right.

One advantage that Casablanca offered over Karachi, from the American housewife's point of view, was that she could pick up certain articles she had grown accustomed to without having to send thousands of miles away for them. Ships, for instance, frequently visited Casablanca, and if we went aboard before the customs officers sealed their shops, we could buy cameras, perfumes, watches and other luxury items tax free.

A more permanent source of goods was the commissary at the American Air Force base, which was a twenty-five-mile drive from Casablanca. There we could take the children to see American movies or to buy comic books, and there we could pick up such American staples as milk, ice cream and even potato chips. The commissary even sold squishy American bread, which many Americans, living on the base, preferred to that wonderful French bread in town. This is a curious aspect of American bases overseas. The wives of servicemen stationed there often isolated themselves in that "Little America," never venturing into the "dirty" world outside, never coming into any closer contact with the sensuous North African sights and smells. It was as if they had been living all the time in some sequestered Midwestern housing development. I felt sorry for them.

With such a variety of foods at my disposal, I cooked with a relish I have seldom experienced before or since. Our kitchen in Casablanca was not as uncomfortably hot as it had been in Karachi, and I used a good gas stove rather than the kerosene one on which we had done our cooking there. Making the prospect of cooking all the more pleasurable for me was the presence of a houseboy, who cleaned up for me afterward.

In contrast to the many servants we had around us in Karachi, we hired only the houseboy and later a nanny to look after the baby in Casablanca. A nanny doesn't quite tell the story. We went through several of them before finding a wonderful German girl named Hannie Eckels. Hannie was young and pretty, and was engaged to an American GI from Tennessee. We became good friends. When Hannie and her GI were married I went out and bought all the flowers I could for ten dollars, which was more flowers than I had ever seen gathered together before in my life. The house was full of them. We filled every vase in the church, too, and stuck the leftovers into a couple of diaper buckets.

The Hoyts, in Casablanca, were a two-servant but a one-car family. Before leaving Karachi we had ordered a Mercedes to be delivered to us in Casablanca. The delivery was delayed, and the car did not reach us until Christmas, when Michael was able to give it to me as a "present." Meanwhile we had been driving around in a huge ancient black Renault 15CV, the "gangster" car, with front-wheel drive. It consumed enormous quantities of gasoline. Once I neglected to keep my eye on the fuel gauge, and the car coughed to a stop many miles outside of town. Fortunately, I was able to flag down a helpful motorist. Another time I used my wits to better advantage. A policeman stopped me for speeding on the road to Rabat. I explained to him that the old heap couldn't possibly have exceeded the speed limit. I still don't know whether it was the policeman's gallantry or his credulity that prompted him to send me on my way with just a warning and a smile.

11 ★
Diplomatic Life in Casablanca

Our two years in Casablanca flew by, partly because many of the aspects of living abroad were now familiar to us, and partly because Michael's new responsibilities threw us into contact with dozens of diverting people. Often he was busy writing reports, of course, reports on both the general framework of the Moroccan economy and on the reliability of individual firms in the area. As the Consulate's economic and commercial officer, Michael was expected to be of whatever help he could to American businessmen and their interests around Casablanca. This kept him in constant touch with both businessmen and politicians, and sent him on frequent trips into the countryside. What was the economic condition of the country? What was the central government doing to encourage investment? What was the situation in the local mining industry? American businessmen, investing in local industry or dealing with local firms, wanted to know, and here Michael could advise them. More specifically, he was able to introduce an American, perhaps new to the country, to the local politicians or business leaders who might be helpful to the man in his work.

After he had served in Casablanca for a time, and especially after the Consulate's administrative officer left for another post, Michael's duties were broadened. On different occasions he handled tasks essential to each of several branches of Consulate work—administrative, consular, political, economic and commercial. Some of these duties may seem relatively unimportant if one sees a Foreign Service officer as dealing only with weighty negotiations between rival governments, but they mean much to the people involved. Perhaps it was simply a tourist who had arrived in Casablanca bearing a letter from his Congressman, which asked the Consulate to do everything in its power to make his stay there pleasant and informative. In that event, Michael dropped his other duties temporarily to take the tourist and his wife sightseeing about the city.

Or perhaps a dignitary appeared suddenly in town. This was the case when Senator Frank Church of Idaho arrived in Casablanca with a large party of people during his African tour. They asked for a Moroccan dinner, and Michael had to move with some haste to arrange it. He called a friend who owned a restaurant downtown and made reservations for the senator and his party to enjoy a typically fine local dinner.

A consular post which happens to be a seaport may also be called upon to play host to visiting Navy personnel when a ship ties up there. While we were in Casablanca the cruiser *Springfield,* the flagship of the Sixth Fleet, arrived and paid what is called in diplomatic language a "naval visit." On board was Admiral George W. Anderson, who later became Chief of Naval Operations. The event caused quite a stir. For weeks beforehand we made elaborate preparations for what was only a three-day visit. Parties were arranged for every evening, at which we entertained the entire crew. Finding enough girls to act as dancing partners for the thousand-man crew was one of my jobs. On the climactic evening we invited a number of officers to our home, and later went on to nearby parties, where Consulate couples were entertaining other groups.

Occasionally Michael dealt with people who were to play a part in our life at a later date. Among these businessmen was Arnold Hartpence, who became the head of Mobil Oil operations in the Congo. And by one of those recurring threads which one follows in the Foreign Service, Michael's consul-general in Casablanca was Tommy Tomlinson, who had been the last United States consul-general in Leopoldville before the Congo received its independence and the post was elevated to an Embassy. Bill Schaufele worked with Michael in the Consulate and later was the consul in the eastern Congo city of Bukavu.

There were frequent calls from Americans in distress. As a rule, most of these distress calls are handled by a Consulate on an unofficial basis, as when an American citizen walks in and confides that he is dead broke and doesn't know where his next meal is coming from. The officer he speaks to may sympathize with the man's story and dig down into his own pocket to advance him enough money to get back on his feet. When the distressed man disappears and is never heard from again, the officer who "lent" him the money has been the loser. To keep one man from assuming all the risks, the Consulate officers and a group of American businessmen in Casablanca contributed to a fund to provide against such calls for immediate financial assistance.

Sometimes the consul can be of help in a more difficult case. While Michael was in Casablanca, two American servicemen were arrested by the local police on charges which might have had serious consequences for them. The charge concerned the black-market exchange of currency, and the Moroccan authorities were determined to prosecute the men. Michael investigated the case and discovered to his satisfaction that it was simply a matter of an exchange of money between two friends, neither of whom was making a profit on the deal. The exchange, however, had been witnessed by a Moroccan plainclothesman, who had immediately stepped in and arrested the GI's. Michael, luckily, had friends in the

Moroccan justice department. He made an appointment with a couple of them to explain the case. His friendships profited the GI's. The authorities accepted Michael's explanation; the charges were dropped and the servicemen released.

Sometimes a diplomat's duties expose him to the risk of personal injury (a risk we were to appreciate in greater intensity somewhat later). After the death of the Moroccan King Mohammed V in February, 1961, there were public demonstrations of mourning. The emotions aroused by the death of the well-loved monarch threatened to flare into riots if there was a dispute over the succession. It was part of Michael's job to submit a report on the course of the demonstrations in Casablanca. I remember the day he went downtown to keep tabs on the surging crowds, skirting around the skirmishes and staying close to the protective shelter of buildings. At other times there were more serious riots over the Algerian and Mauretanian questions. For the first time I became aware that a diplomat's wife may have more to worry about than the supervision of native servants and the prevalence of mildew.

A major catastrophe struck Morocco while we were there. On March 1, 1960, an earthquake devastated the coastal city of Agadir, 250 miles south of Casablanca. It was estimated that 12,000 people lost their lives. American aid was sent by air to the disaster victims, while all of us in Casablanca collected food and clothing to be shipped to the city. I sorted and boxed clothing that had been donated (my most vivid memory of those wild days was handling the filthy clothes sent in by "generous" people; it was horrible). Once we had sorted the clothes, we discovered that there were no paper bags or boxes in which we could ship them to Agadir. Michael called the American Air Force base outside Casablanca, and got speedy results. The Air Force sent us a truckload of collapsible boxes, and included masking tape and markers so that the packed boxes could be marked according to the size and type of clothing they contained.

Later Michael went to Agadir to investigate the economic consequences of the earthquake. There was, in particular, a heavily damaged orange-packing plant that was partially owned by an American firm. He returned with emotions not usually associated with a "business" trip, because he had spent some time in the city before the earthquake. What had been a bustling little port was now virtually dead. The lovely old hotel he had stayed in earlier was now merely an indistinguishable heap among the general rubble.

It was about this time that the African nations were emerging in a great rush for independence. Almost every week seemed to bring news of another bright new country taking its first steps on its own with all the pride and disorder which usually accompanies such an event. The State Department sent out to all its embassies and consulates a request for volunteers to man the new posts, many of them in isolated, primitive and dangerous regions, which this situation demanded. Michael, whose interest in African affairs was by now confirmed, volunteered for one of them. However, because he was already serving in Africa, he was not taken.

I remember that shortly after Michael had volunteered for one of these "hardship" posts, an AID (Agency for International Development) officer arrived in Casablanca. He had come from Leopoldville after witnessing the disorders following independence there in 1960. He told us frightening stories of the breakdown of law and order, of the violence against both blacks and whites, of senseless murders and burnings, of torture and rape. The stories shocked us at the time, but they seemed, from the point of view of our settled and opulent life in Casablanca, to be the reports of uproar in a distant part of the earth. I was to recall these stories in vivid detail four years later.

12 ★
Enter Evans Hoyt

There was an event of a more personal nature at this time which helped to take my mind off the disturbing news from the south. I was pregnant. Birth in America today assumes an almost casual air, but my fourth child was to be born in a strange city, thousands of miles from where I had given birth to his brothers and sister.

Originally I had planned to have my baby in the more familiar surroundings of the hospital at the American Air Force base at Nouasseur. That plan had been killed by the obstetrician there, who would not agree to induce labor for me. He didn't approve of the procedure, he said. The distance to the base from where we lived was twenty-five miles. Since each of the other children had seemed in a great hurry to be born, I did not think it wise to take the chance of rushing out there for a last-minute delivery. So I made plans to have the baby in a private clinic, operated by a French doctor, in Casablanca itself.

When the time came, Michael drove me to the clinic. The first two floors of the building were exclusively for abortions, which is a popular means of birth control among the Europeans in Morocco. Only the third, or top, floor of the clinic was given over to simple maternity cases. I went into labor shortly after arriving there. Everything went so quickly that they did not have time to move me into the delivery room (and that American obstetrician had wanted me to drive twenty-five miles!) Michael remained in the room to translate for me.

But there was a moment of panic. The umbilical cord had wrapped itself around the baby's neck and was slowly choking him. The doctor moved swiftly and cut the cord, then applied mouth-to-mouth artificial respiration. The next thing I knew I had a beautiful baby boy beside me. We named him Evans.

The doctor who had saved the child was nonetheless embarrassed by the makeshift conditions under which the birth had taken place. He made Michael go with him to the delivery room so he could see how it had been cleaned up and the anesthetics made ready for my arrival. But the doctor balked when we asked to have Evans circumcised. "You Americans want to cut off everything," he told Michael.

The doctor who operated the clinic proved more responsive. He agreed to perform the circumcision himself. On the appointed day Michael came to the hospital and was invited by the doctor into the operating room, which was next to mine. Afterward he came in and told me about it.

"I guess the doctor had an appointment, because he seemed to be in a hurry," Michael said. "His wife was in there, too, and both of them were dressed for a party. She stood off to one side while he went to work."

"Wasn't there anybody to help him?" I asked.

Michael shook his head. "The doctor just took off his jacket and shirt and put on a rubber apron to cover his dress trousers. He went in and out of the operating room a couple of times. And all the time he worked he was puffing on a cigarette, like he was wrapping packages."

I should have been shocked, I suppose, but I couldn't help smiling. "Was everything all right?"

Michael nodded. "A real slick job," he said.

And so I returned to the normal life of a diplomat's wife abroad. The Consulate had a number of projects under way at the time. I often helped out by repairing old toys for the local orphanage, for instance. Even with an infant in the house, I found that I still had a great deal of freedom from the ordinary household chores. The house was easy to care for, the kitchen easy to cook in (especially with that houseboy standing over my shoulder to tidy up afterward). Because Casablanca had a number of good hotels, we were not asked to put up as many visitors as we ordinarily would in a city with more primitive facilities. I even found it easier to care for myself than I had at home in the States. There were excellent French hairdressers nearby, and I was able to run over to them and have my hair washed and set for about a dollar. And once the people there got to know me, I could go in every day and have it combed free of charge.

My social life improved as my French lessons progressed, although my French teacher, Monique Bourreaud, was so charming, we perhaps spent more time talking than learning. Some of our closest friends in Casablanca were Moroccans, and we were often invited to their homes for dinner. It was always a fresh experience. There were exotic dishes like *couscous,* a fine grain farina which one picked up with the hands and rolled into little balls before popping them into the mouth. And great pigeon pies, two and three feet in diameter, with powdered sugar sprinkled over the crust. And the delicious lamb dishes, the hostess selecting the choice pieces for her guests and passing them along with her fingers. (I remember one awful evening taking a piece of lamb from the hostess and noticing that her fingernails were positively filthy. I nearly died!)

Although the women of the lower class were still veiled, those of the upper class had won their freedom. This step was largely the result of the efforts of one remarkable woman: Lalla Aisha, King Mohammed V's eldest daughter. She was a warm-hearted but unpredictable woman, and much of the high life of both Casablanca and Rabat (the capital, some fifty miles away) revolved around her. Michael and I had made her acquaintance, and had grown very fond of her. One evening, just as we were preparing to leave for some sort of function, one of Lalla Aisha's friends appeared at our front door. The princess, she told us, wanted us to be her guests that evening at a performance of the Russian ballet. We had already accepted another invitation —but who could refuse the invitation of a princess? Certainly not a Midwestern girl.

And much to our surprise the princess came to *us*. She appeared with some friends to pick us up and take us to the theater. The children came down the stairs shyly, to greet their first real live princess. Other friends of Lalla Aisha appeared, and we took a long time to leave. We were late, of course, for the ballet. It was one time in my life that I was not embarrassed to arrive late for a public performance.

Another day we drove to Rabat for a dancing party given by the princess. It must have been winter. I can fix the time of year because the winter was an especially lively season in Casablanca. The entertainment here differed markedly from that in Karachi, for the new freedom permitted Moslem women to dance, as well as dress in Western fashion (Pakistani women seldom danced.) In Casablanca the festive occasion was a buffet dinner and a dance. And there were concerts all winter, since the city was on the European concert tour. The United States Information Agency, under our Cultural Exchange Program, brought many prominent American artists to the city, and others, such as the Budapest String Quartet, were brought in by local impresarios.

Yet year round there was much to occupy us. The beach was nearby. If the Atlantic Ocean water was chilly, as it was for a good part of the year, there were a number of fresh- and salt-water pools just behind the beaches. And the restaurants along the beach were among the best at which we've ever eaten. I remember one of them particularly—La Mer—which was run by a French couple. It sat up in the rocks high above the beach, and there we could sit at a table and watch a storm move in darkly across the sea and send the waves crashing into the spotlighted rocks below us. We always ordered the onion soup, which came in bowls as large as tureens, and the fish. This dinner, with wine, coffee and, of course, the marvelous bread and the wonderful service, cost only a couple of dollars a person.

On holidays we visited other Moroccan cities. There was a trip to the old religious center of Fez, and two trips to Marrakech, that favorite haunt of Winston Churchill. There we would sit at a café in the main square, watching the people pour past and expecting to see everyone we had ever met. A dense latticework of branches hung over the narrow streets of the *souks* (markets) and filtered the heat from the sun overhead while scattering its light in dazzling patterns across the sidewalk. Here, too, in Marrakech, were the tombs of the

Saadian kings, tucked away in the most peaceful setting I have ever seen.

Our most ambitious excursion turned out to be the unexpected gift of the local utilities company. We knew from the beginning that electricity was expensive in Casablanca. Yet we used a lot of it, particularly because the house was heated by electric radiators. But no one came to read the meter. We shuddered at the prospect of receiving the long-delayed bill. By our calculations it would amount to over three hundred dollars. Still no one came. Finally, after the meter had turned full cycle, a reader appeared. The meter showed only a negligible reading, and the bill amounted to only a few francs. Unashamedly, we took the money we had put away to pay the electric bill and went across to Spain.

There we spent two wonderful weeks, touring by car from Seville to Madrid, and from there to the lovely medieval town of Casceres, with streets so narrow one could touch the walls on each side with outstretched fingers. This was the home of the Conquistadores. After a flare-up of feudal bickering, these people were sent from Casceres to the New World, where they grew wealthy. Returning at last to Casceres, they built the magnificent homes which remain the town's chief glory. Finally, we drove on to the peaceful Moroccan coastal town of Mogador, all blue and white in the sun, criss-crossed by tiny streets—a miniature fairyland.

13 ★
School and Suburbia

We had had a taste of Africa—the fringe of Africa, to be sure, smelling and tasting a good deal like the Near East and sounding, in the accents of its drawing rooms and the hubbub of its boulevards, like Western Europe. This northern rim of the continent really has little in common with what lies below. An immense desert has proved nearly impenetrable. Yet the links are there, and they are ancient. The Moslem world was as far ahead of the European in establishing contact with the black African as it was in brewing coffee or cultivating tulips.

We were destined to penetrate that huge dark land that lies below the Sahara, but when we left Casablanca we didn't know it. Michael, of course, hoped for further duty in Africa. But first, following our two years' assignment in Casablanca, there would be the usual home leave and then, for Michael, a period of advanced study.

A Foreign Service officer's formal education doesn't end with his appointment to the corps. He is always, really, in training, getting part of his education on the job (a diplomat's first assignment is simply an extension of his training, as Michael's two-year apprenticeship in Karachi was). But the Foreign Service is a competitive organization in a very real sense. It is not a lifetime sinecure. When a diplomat does not continue to advance up the ladder of the service through promotions, that is, when he does not continue to increase in value to his service and his country, he is automatically dropped from the ranks. This keeps the Foreign Service always in flux, and its individual members always alert.

Michael, having already chosen to specialize in African affairs, was now ready to go into his subject in greater depth. After our home leave (seeing relatives, renewing friendships, the children spending every waking hour in front of the TV until they wearied of it at last and turned to the radio or the phonograph), Michael was assigned to spend nine months at the graduate school of Northwestern University. The oldest and best-known African studies program in the United States is located at Northwestern. It was there that Michael was sent, rather than to the Foreign Service Institute in Washington, to continue his studies in both economics and African affairs.

If it was "back to school" for Michael, it was back to suburbia for all of us. We settled in Deerfield, Illinois, not far from the university at Evanston. While Michael pored over his books, I ferried the children to school or to Cub Scout meetings, baked brownies and shopped in supermarkets. We spoke of Little League baseball games and of trips to the Chicago museums. The bazaars of Karachi and the elegant Moslem homes of Casablanca seemed very far away. Intensifying the sense of unreality was the ominous rumble of bigotry around us as Deerfield undertook an experimental integration program. I had mingled with friends of other races in Pakistan and Morocco (and was to make good friends with those of still another race in the Congo) and here I was forced to avoid the nasty prattle of suburban racemongers. Ironically, Michael, wrapped up in his studies of an area where so many races sprang up, dispersed and peopled the world, was spared a great deal of this local nonsense.

Then, when Michael's orders finally came, we were sharply disappointed. We had been all set for an assignment somewhere in Africa, preferably below the Sahara. But the country to which Michael had been ordered to report had nothing to do with Africa: Israel!

So while Michael fretted, I packed and began to ship our belongings to Tel Aviv. We sold the Mercedes, ordering a Rambler instead because it would be difficult to find parts for the German-manufactured Mercedes in Israel. I have seldom heard Michael complain. But now he believed, as we all did, that it had been a terrible waste to send him to school for almost a year to concentrate on African studies, and then at the last minute assign him to a post where those studies would be of little use to him.

Michael made up his mind to try to have the assignment changed. While he flew to Washington to talk to people in the State Department, I took the children to my sister's home in Boonville, Indiana. There I waited for definite word from Michael. He would call me every day. "We've been assigned to Constantine, Algeria," he said the first time he called. The next day he called to say that we were headed for Johannesburg, South Africa. The next day it was some place else. I couldn't stand it.

"I don't care where we go," I told him. "Just let's *go!*"

And finally we knew. It was to be Leopoldville, in the Congo. They had seen the illogic of the previous assignment. Frantically we sent wires, trying to stop the shipment of our belongings to Israel and reroute them to Leopoldville. In the trunks was clothing intended for the hot, dry climate of Israel; we had little equipment for the humid equatorial region for which we were bound. We even heard that Mercedes parts were easier to come by in the Congo than those for a Rambler, but it was too late to change the order.

There was still some packing to be finished. Many people in the Foreign Service leave behind their best silver and other valuable possessions when they are sent to a tropical post. Michael and I, however, enjoy our possessions. We use them constantly, and like to keep them with us wherever we go. So I packed up our silver and sent that along to Leopoldville (some of it, including a sterling silver set for twelve, was to be appropriated for use on the tables of Simba leaders, but I'm not sorry we took them with us). The children and I joined Michael in Washington, and there we got our shots for the Congo: typhoid, typhus, smallpox, diphtheria, yellow fever, cholera and the bubonic plague. We were somewhat distressed when we learned we were to receive a shot for the bubonic plague, but there had been a recent death in the Congo from this horrible disease, and although it developed that the victim was a doctor experimenting with plague germs, it was best not to take chances.

We sailed from New York again on the *Independence.* Our destination was Naples, where we would disembark, make our way to Rome and fly from there to the Congo. Happily, our boat touched briefly at Casablanca before entering the Mediterranean, and we were granted six delightful hours ashore. Hannie, our young German maid, and her GI husband were at the dock to meet us and look after the children. Other friends were there awaiting our arrival. The consul-general, Tommy Tomlinson, and his wife, Gay, were on the dock, along with Larry and Peggy O'Hana. We were rushed to a reception in our honor.

Michael and I crowded a lot of fun into those few hours and revived a lot of memories. Suddenly it was time to return to the ship. Michael and I separated, he going with the Tomlinsons in their car, and I with the

O'Hanas. Larry insisted on stopping at his place to pick up a couple of bottles of that good Moroccan rosé wine as a going-away present for Michael. The stop took longer than we had expected. Now we were rushing to catch the boat before it pulled out, Larry turning the corners on two wheels, the men laughing, the ladies in the back seat screeching in fright.

When we arrived at the dock, the main gangplank had already been removed and the crew was preparing to take down the small one. Hannie, worried that the boat would sail with her still aboard, had come ashore, leaving the children on deck. Michael was standing on the dock too, looking distraught and arguing with a couple of men from the shipping line.

"I'm not going aboard until Jo comes," he kept insisting.

I came up behind him, laughing, and we both skipped aboard as the small gangplank came down.

If it was not quite as delightful, the rest of our trip seemed equally hectic. There was a stop at Majorca, where we toured the city in a horse-drawn carriage, and I fell *up* the steps of a church with Evans in my arms, nearly breaking my leg. There was our arrival in Naples, where we asked for two taxis to take us and our luggage to the railroad station. But a voluble cab driver insisted he could take all of us in one cab, piling our luggage and a baby bed on the roof and sitting Reed on top of some other bags next to him in the front seat. The rest of us squeezed into the back. The cab driver set off for the station, blowing his horn and waving to his friends so that they would be sure to notice the tremendous load he had taken aboard. I felt as if I were part of a Mardi Gras parade.

And there was the train trip to Rome, terribly expensive because we had not brought our own food along and were obliged to eat in the dining car. Lunch for the six of us cost over forty dollars.

In Rome we stayed with a friend of Michael's family. After a week's sightseeing we boarded the plane for Leopoldville. It seems a shame, in a way, for us to have touched the shores of Africa in a ship and then withdrawn to Europe—then make another rush at it from the air. One should approach Africa more leisurely, watch from the rail of a ship as it takes shape in the distance. One might then be better prepared for it. But now we were wrenched from modern Europe, from the Eternal City itself, and shortly were dropped down, pell-mell, into a place which seemed even more timeless than Rome itself.

14 ★
The Congo

We landed, as usual when we are arriving in a strange city, at night. The flight had been uneventful, the Sahara rolling away under us like an interminable sheet of blank paper and then the clouds closing in near the equator, obscuring everything. We descended from the night sky to land on a pitch-dark airstrip at Leopold-ville. A few bulbs could be seen burning dimly inside the terminal, but outside, the lights had given way to economy.

The Congolese customs people are notorious for their strict adherence to regulations. Diamond smugglers are ordinarily their bugbear, but we had heard many stories from Westerners of the indignities to which they had been subjected by newly appointed and sensitive Congolese officials. Much to our relief there was a couple, John and Polly Clingerman, from the American Embassy, waiting for us at the airport gate; John was later to become the American consul in Stanleyville, where Michael succeeded him.

We were a bit on edge, I suppose. There had been all those terrible stories of violence at the time of the Congo's independence. But now we passed through the gate with a minimum of difficulty. I searched for the source of my uneasiness, but without success. Customs . . . local authority deferring to American prestige . . . perhaps a touch of dinginess here and there, but nothing mysterious, nothing frightening. We drove with the Clingermans past the tall modern buildings, through the wide deserted streets. The Congo, I assured myself, was just another diplomatic post.

We had arrived in this place at a fascinating and, as it turned out, dangerous period. The Congo is an immense country, covering an area as large as that portion of the United States east of the Mississippi River. The equator runs through the northern part of the country, so that the climate is hot and humid (although it is not all jungle, since there are great stretches of savanna and, in the east, even snow-covered mountains—the fabulous "Mountains of the Moon").

It was Henry Morton Stanley, the explorer and journalist, who reported to the world in the 1870's the story of an incredible trip down the Congo River and an appraisal (his own) of that region's nearly infinite potential. King Leopold of the Belgians was the first European monarch to take advantage of that information.

He commissioned Stanley to undertake further journeys in the Congo and conclude treaties with local tribal chiefs. Plans were also laid to build the railroad that was to link Leopoldville upriver with Matadi on the coast and create a vital transportation system along the Congo River, which was navigable up to Stanleyville on the edge of Stanley Falls. Then, as the first step in an almost unparalleled epic of greed and cruelty, Leopold formed the Congo Free State and set himself up as both the supreme monarch of the state and the chief stockholder in the managing company. Here in the Belgian Congo occurred the classic drama of colonial exploitation. Leopold sold immense tracts of land as concessions to commercial companies, which were obliged to exploit the land and its people to recoup their original investments. The black man's portion was sweat and blood; dying, he handed on to his conquerors the country's treasures.

To a world which had come to accept the doctrine of progress in man's condition, the gradual revelation of the natives' suffering in Congolese mines and plantations came as a disturbing warning. Primitive brutality had survived centuries of civilizing influences in Europe and was there beneath the surface, ready to rouse itself when the proper chord was touched. Belgium was swept by reform. Its parliament took the personal management of the Congo out of the king's hands and stipulated that it be administered by a governor-general, appointed by the king, with the advice and consent of the parliament. Though their condition was ameliorated, the Congolese gained only a minute share of their country's wealth and none of the responsibilities of government. The interest of the big European landowners still took precedence over every other administrative concern.

The Congo remained a free trade area, a status it had secured under King Leopold, when as a concession to the other European powers to secure his sovereignty over the country, he had agreed not to establish trade barriers. The country's natural resources were legendary. Minerals such as copper, tin and manganese were abundant. Agricultural products such as coffee, cotton and palm oil flourished with proper care. Yet the entire economy was based on European investment and European personnel. Africans occupied only the lowest jobs, as clerks and laborers. As independence approached they began to sift through into minor supervisory positions, acting as team chiefs in factories and on plantations. But the African was excluded from management as entirely as he was from government.

In 1960, with the arrival of independence from Belgium, the Congo's economy suffered a sharp setback. The Congolese were untrained for leadership in either government or industry (university educations, which had been open to some Africans under French and British colonial rule, were almost completely denied to the Congolese by their Belgian rulers). The pull-out of trained Europeans left an enormous vacuum in management. The feeble central government was not able to contain the revolt of the Congolese army immediately after independence. Areas within the Congo, such as Moishe Tshombe's Katanga and Albert Kalongi's South Kasai, seceded from this government. In order to protect its citizens, who were at the mercy of uncontrolled mobs, the Belgians dropped paratroopers and restored order in the cities. President Joseph Kasavubu and Prime Minister Patrice Lumumba, both of whom had led rival political parties before independence, were again at odds. In desperation, the central government asked the United Nations to intervene. Firmly backed by the United States, the UN poured troops and technicians into the Congo.

Lumumba, however, chose not to co-operate with the United Nations forces which had arrived in the country to restore stability to the government. He elected instead to deal unilaterally with the Soviet Union, asking its counsel and assistance. In September, 1960, President Kasavubu dismissed Lumumba as Prime Minister. Lumumba defied him. At this chaotic moment Colonel Joseph Mobutu, the army's chief of staff, intervened and formed a government of "commissioners." (Mobutu was to intervene during another crisis five years later.) Turning on the Soviet technicians and diplomats, who he felt were a source of trouble in the Congo, Mobutu ejected them and arrested Lumumba. Shortly afterward Lumumba was sent to Katanga under mysterious circumstances, and his body was discovered later.

Eventually Kasavubu and parliament resumed the reins of government but the situation remained terribly unstable. Followers of the dead Lumumba, who now was hailed as a martyr by Congo leftists, were entrenched in the area around Stanleyville. This city, six hundred air miles northeast of Leopoldville on the Congo River, had been named in honor of the great explorer who first voyaged down the river. (This was the last outpost upriver in Conrad's *Heart of Darkness.*) The Congo remained on the edge of chaos. Secessions and threats of rebellion kept both the government army and the United Nations forces constantly in action. Conferences were optimistically called, then despondently adjourned. Lumumba's followers, under Antoine Gizenga, were subdued at Stanleyville, but Tshombe's troops clashed with government forces in Katanga. While on a mission to attempt to arrange a cease-fire, UN Secretary-General Dag Hammarskjold was killed in an airplane accident in Katanga.

It was only in January, 1963, after a nearly interminable succession of conferences, rows and skirmishes, that UN troops rolled back Tshombe's troops and mercenaries to resolve the Katanga secession, and the troubled province rejoined the central government. A measure of stability returned to the Congo. Stanleyville, that hotbed of Communist-inspired rebellion, again took its place with Leopoldville and Elisabethville in the triumvirate of the new nation's major cities. On June 30, 1964, the United Nations forces withdrew from the

Congo, leaving the government's army (Armée National Congolaise or ANC) hopefully in command.

It was against this unsettled background that Michael, arriving in September, 1962, served as the American Embassy's commercial officer. As such, he was chiefly responsible for the commercial relations between the Congo and the United States. On a general level, he sent back to the State Department in Washington various reports on the overall economic situation in the Congo, résumés of local trade regulations and periodic suggestions on the opportunities for trade there.

These reports were designed, of course, to help the American businessmen (and there were many) who were interested in doing business with the Congolese. On the other hand, Michael made contacts with Congolese businessmen and encouraged them to trade with American firms. He also worked closely with the AID (Agency for International Development) program that had been established by the United States to make various development loans and grants to the emerging nations. Part of this program provided grants to the Congo under which they could buy American goods, and Michael was necessarily involved in the many ways to make it easier for the Americans to sell and the Congolese to buy. Ultimately, Michael's work contributed to the United States policy in the Congo. That policy was to avert chaos by supporting those elements which promised to promote a stable country.

One of Michael's most satisfying accomplishments

was the Investment Guaranty Agreement signed by the Congo government. Under this agreement American businessmen were able to insure their investments there. Because of the unstable situation in the country, such an agreement was highly desirable if more Americans were to be persuaded to risk their money in local ventures. The agreement was not easy to effect. Michael and Edmund Gullion, the American ambassador, were frustrated time and again, just when it appeared that the Congo government might be ready to sign. Then one evening after Michael had returned from the Embassy, he was summoned to the office of Foreign Minister Justin Bomboko. Ambassador Gullion was also present. The Congo government had agreed to the proposal, and there, late at night, the principals signed their names to the agreement.

Michael's position kept him in close contact with a great number of people. There were American and Congolese businessmen, of course, whom he got to know well, but he also mingled with Belgians, Dutchmen, Englishmen and Frenchmen. Occasionally he was called on to work with diplomats from the other Leopoldville embassies on some aspect of local economic development. And his dealings with representatives of the United Nations enlarged his responsibilities. I remember one day, for instance, when he had a run-in with Robert Gardiner, the Ghanan head of the UN operation in the Congo. During the long crisis in Katanga, Michael wanted to persuade Cyrille Adoula, then the prime minister in the central government, to pay a visit to one of the newly liberated cities there. Such a visit by a high-ranking official, he believed, would inspire confidence in the stability of the government and make a good impression on the local people. Gardiner, however, disagreed. Moving very cautiously, he felt that the situation in Katanga was still too explosive for the prime minister to risk making an appearance. At a meeting with Michael he expressed his displeasure, and hot words were exchanged.

On the whole, Michael's relationships were not only extremely friendly, but many of the businessmen whom he met during his assignment in Leopoldville were to prove helpful at a later time when he needed all the friends he could get. The trips out of Leopoldville that Michael made in connection with his duties were then my chief worry: trips into remote areas where the conditions were very primitive, or, what was worse, where the people might be hostile to both American diplomats and representatives of the Leopoldville government. Yet those trips, to mining centers, plantations, provincial capitals and other vital centers of the Congolese economy, were necessary. Great changes would be needed if the Congo was to prosper. The Belgians, of course, had built the economy chiefly for their own purposes. Vast amounts of copper, for instance, were mined in the Congo, then shipped to Belgium for processing. The finished product was sold elsewhere for the profit of the Belgians. At the time Michael was stationed there, the Congo was in a period of transition, laboriously moving toward that point where it would be able to function as an independent country, rather than as the colony of a distant European nation. Because the Congo would not be a stable country until that transition had been completed, the United States government needed frequent reports on both its extent and its pace. It was Michael's job to prepare those reports.

But it was in Leopoldville that he performed most of his duties. There he prompted the organization of an American Businessmen's Club, at which many valuable ideas were exchanged and discussed. And it was there that Michael labored long and futilely on what a punster might refer to as a "pet" project. I'll simply refer to it as Operation Baby Elephant.

Before Congolese independence, the Lincoln Park Zoo in Chicago had made arrangements with the Stanleyville provincial government to buy a baby elephant for its children's zoo. Lincoln Park officials had even sent a check in full payment for the animal. But negotiations lapsed at the time of independence. The elephant had never been delivered and the money had been swallowed up in the general disorder. When Michael took up his duties at the Embassy he inherited a stout file of correspondence on the matter.

It seemed a simple task, and he set about trying to clear it up. Letters flew, the file expanded. Michael contacted officials in the Congo government, and they agreed to do everything possible to locate and ship a baby elephant to the Lincoln Park Zoo. Nothing happened. Michael went so far as to bring the matter to the attention of the agricultural minister, who agreed to make a "gift" of the elephant to the zoo.

But the gesture remained just that. The Congo government was fighting for its very existence. The task of capturing and delivering a baby elephant proved, to Michael's frustration, to be more than it could cope with.

15 ⋆
Getting Settled Again

Like the Plains Indians, I had become proficient in the procedure of hurriedly assembling or dismantling a home. If it was not a nightly task, it was certainly by now a frequent one. In Leopoldville, as in most of the other cities where we had lived, I was set back in trying to establish a home by the simple fact that I couldn't find one big enough for us; housing shortages seem to be universal. For three months the six of us crowded into an apartment in downtown Leopoldville. Above us lived Lew and Connie Hoffacker. He had been the American consul in Elisabethville during Tshombe's Katanga secession and had experienced what it could be like to live isolated in a hostile community, for the United States had been outspoken against the secession. Finally I located a house on the city's outskirts, a ten-mile drive from downtown. It apparently had been overlooked because many people were afraid to live that far from the center of Leopoldville.

The Embassy rented the house from an American businessman (he sold soft drinks) named Maurice Alhadeff, who later became a good friend of ours. Pleasant and roomy, the house was a duplex. On the other side lived a Belgian banker, his Hungarian wife and their six children. Our part of the house was illuminated —that is the word which best describes it—by thirteen large French windows, painted orange, blue, yellow and other bright colors, but subdued by me to a uniform white. There was a massive fireplace in the living room. Outside, the two families shared a small pool, several lush shade trees and a yard large enough to contain the ten children and several pets.

The outlook was almost theatrical. Our house stood on high ground overlooking the Congo River, which generally flowed a rich muddy red. At certain times of the year, however, the muddy flow was obscured by a spectacular covering of white and violet water hyacinths. And at twilight during the dry season there began to form a fiery canopy over the dark river and hills. The source of this glow was the fires which were lit by farmers to clear the land and fertilize the soil. Often they roared out of control through the tall grass in the countryside. Great mushroom clouds of smoke were visible in the early evening. With the coming of darkness the fires grew brighter, and could be seen to cover a front as broad as fifty miles. Sometimes the fires appeared on the Leopoldville side of the river, and at other times they flared up from the Brazzaville side. Then it seemed as if the mountains themselves had gone up in flames.

Life for a Western family in Leopoldville, like that in Karachi, seemed to demand a retinue of servants. I learned that Leopoldville servants had a kind of unofficial union, and they did not work more than eight hours at a time. I hired two shifts, a houseboy who worked from six A.M. until two P.M., and another who came in at noon and stayed with us until after dinner. We paid each of them twenty-five dollars a month. We also had a yard boy, a laundry boy and a night watchman.

There were the usual problems that came up when we tried to break them in. On one chilly evening Michael asked the houseboy to set a fire for us in the fireplace so that it would be ready when we returned home from a reception. Fortunately, the houseboy didn't light the fire before we came back. We came in to find that mammoth fireplace stuffed full of logs—there must have been a half-cord of wood in there! Michael took off his jacket and began the laborious job of dislodging them, one by one.

And the laundry boy! He came dutifully six days a week, but though we provided him with an electric washer and dryer, he couldn't keep up with our laundry. To say that he was slow is an understatement. And there was the night watchman. He slept so soundly that when we returned late at night from some function, Michael couldn't rouse him even by repeatedly blowing the car horn. Finally Michael would have to get out of the car and open the gates himself. It was a joy to find someone who enjoyed a night's sleep so completely as our watchman did.

We also hired a driver, who turned out to be a better bargain than some of our other servants. Jean drove the children to school, and Michael to work. It was almost a full-time job, because the children attended the American Baptist Mission School, originally set up for missionaries' children but bursting at its seams now with the American population explosion in Leopoldville: the families of army officers, diplomats, AID officials and businessmen. The school was seven miles from our home. The Embassy, where Michael went every morning, was even farther. The Rambler, which we had worried about for a while, held up very well, except for its tires. We wore out three or four sets on Leopoldville's miserable roads.

Jean also helped me considerably by attending to the green-market shopping. Shopping for meat was a different matter. At the big markets everything was encrusted by flies, so that you had to brush them away with your hand to examine the quality of the meat beneath them. It was not polite to ask the hostess at a party who her butcher was; she might not want to tell you. Eventually I found a butcher shop downtown where the meat was properly cared for. Long lines formed when meat was available, and it was not practicable to send a servant to stand in line for you. In-

variably he came back empty-handed, after being ignored by the butchers. At first I had to go myself and
wait in line for two hours or more before being served.
After a while I got to know the butcher and fared much
better (particularly after I gave him a bottle of whiskey
for Christmas).

I encountered other problems in assembling and preparing our food. We ordered flour by the case from Den-
mark. Almost always it arrived full of weevils. Here the
advice of a friend saved me a spasm of hand-wringing,
for she suggested that I strain it through a nylon stock-
ing. The rice, which also arrived full of bugs, demanded
a different solution. We simply waited until we were
ready to cook it, then dropped it into hot water. As the
bugs came wriggling to the surface, we scooped them
off.

But these were minor problems. We were grateful that
we were able to buy such items, bugs and all. In the so-
called "supermarket," meats and vegetables were often
not to be found at any price. The disorders following
independence had so disrupted the country's economic
life that serious food shortages developed. Salt and sugar were extremely scarce and sometimes could be
bought only on the black market. I can remember walking into a supermarket and finding the shelves bare except for cartons of Toni Home Permanents lying about
in inexplicable profusion. At Christmas, when we were
looking for goodies to put in the children's stockings,
we had to take the ferry across the Congo River to Braz-

zaville (in the former French Congo) to buy apples. Even there, the apples cost us $1.25 apiece.

Keeping house in a place like the Congo is not only an organizational experience, it is a combative one. We always had to be careful—about what we ate, where we went, what we let the children do. Much of our equipment (our many medicines, for instance) was on hand simply to defend ourselves against the country's natural dangers.

One valuable appliance was a dryer. We had brought it because we had been told that there is a fly in the Congo which lays its eggs in clothing. While hatching, the larvae are likely to burrow into whatever human skin happens to be next to the clothing. These larvae are small worms, looking like skinned caterpillars, and they are very annoying. But if one's clothes have been placed in a dryer for a time before being worn, any eggs which have found their way into them will become overheated and fail to hatch. The children completely escaped the scourge of the little larvae; only Michael was a victim. On one of our excursions to the beach, he carelessly left his bath towel lying on the ground. Some of the larvae must have become attached first to the towel and then to Michael. He had an awfully unpleasant time of it.

At the beach one also had to beware of slightly larger predators. The beach, you see, was really a sandbar in the Congo River. And in the Congo River, just as in Kipling's "great gray green greasy Limpopo River, all set about with fever trees," one is likely to encounter crocodiles. For the children, who had been swimming in the Arabian Sea off Karachi and the Atlantic Ocean off Casablanca, this was an entirely new experience. They would paddle around in the water, and if an unidentified object was sighted, everybody would set up an excited hullabaloo, and the kids would scoot for the shore. Michael was more successful in evading the crocodiles than he was the fly larvae.

The children likewise escaped the more serious diseases one is likely to be threatened with in the tropics, and for that we were very thankful. A friend of ours contracted hepatitis there and was taken to a local hospital, where she was supposed to receive glucose. Instead, during the course of intravenous feeding, she was given a saline solution (salt is not prescribed for hepatitis victims) and nearly died before being removed to the sanctuary of the UN hospital.

On another occasion our night boy complained of severe stomach pains. Michael took one look at him and ordered Jean to drive him to the local hospital. In a little while the chauffeur returned with the boy, who was still in obvious pain.

"What happened?" Michael demanded. "Why did you bring him back so soon?"

Jean explained. It seems he had taken the boy to the hospital, where his condition had been diagnosed as a strangulated hernia. But the people there had told him to go home and rest, and then return the next week for an operation. Michael put the boy back in the car at once and drove him to the Lovanium Hospital. There they operated on him almost as soon as they got his clothes off.

Our section was called Binza, and, as I have said, it was some distance from downtown Leopoldville. Banditry was a prime topic of conversation among our neighbors, and occasionally we spent uneasy moments when we learned of some particular outrage. Nearby, some bandits had stopped a British couple late one night by placing a log in the road. They had pulled them from the car, raped the woman and beaten the man savagely. In another incident, a housewife had been raped. The police managed to round up one gang. It was said that the gang leader, who had escaped from prison several times, had his Achilles tendon cut by the police to immobilize him. And to make an example of the culprits, the authorities arranged a public hanging, selecting one member of the gang as the victim. Our driver attended the spectacle. When he returned, I overheard his grisly account of it to the children. Apparently the authorities had neglected to tie the victim's feet, so that whenever the trap door was opened, he spread his legs and managed to prop himself up against the sides of the scaffold. Finally he had to be strangled. "His tongue was hanging out just like this!" Jean was telling the children. I had to break in and disperse the fascinated audience.

During the spring before we left, there were political bombings in town. A curfew was imposed, and people were warned to keep off the streets between six P.M. and six A.M. We even arranged curfew parties, where the guests arrived before six in the evening and stayed all night.

One of our friends nearly fell victim to the mounting tension. As he was driving to the airport one day, someone darted out in front of the car. Our friend couldn't stop in time, and ran the man down, killing him. A crowd surrounded the car almost immediately, threatening the driver with death. He jumped out of the car and ran. The crowd, unappeased, stuffed the car with dry grass and set fire to it, while our friend watched helplessly from behind a distant fence. Soon European drivers were instructed to leave the scene of an accident, for their own good. Otherwise, crowds gathered and were likely to destroy either the car or its driver.

But violence and instability seemed no more threatening than in any other world capital, and life in Leopoldville could be very pleasant. After Michael's working day, which often was very long, we entertained, or were entertained, by others. Each diplomatic post has its own complexities. Leopoldville was no exception. There was a considerable missionary population in the Congo, and of course we welcomed the missionaries and their families into our home. But we spent more than one anxious moment trying to decide what to do about the liquor problem. The feelings of American missionaries and diplomats on this question are just as far apart as they can be, and sometimes we had to use extraordinary discretion when entertaining large numbers of both groups. If liquor was a problem, popcorn was not. It was an especially popular offering at every party in Leopoldville, among the foreign guests as well as among the Americans.

Michael's work as the Embassy's commercial officer brought us into the city's business community, and we spent many wonderful evenings with these people: Americans, Belgians, Congolese, Portuguese, French, Germans, and so many others that our dinner parties must have sounded like a Berlitz school gone mad. One heard all sorts of tongues spoken, including several African dialects.

One of our favorite people from this group was Thomas Tumba, a Congolese who was the vice-president of the most important brewery in Leopoldville. There was a kind of twinkle in his eye that attracted others to him. He loved to talk to us about his trips to inspect major breweries in the United States, which Michael had arranged for him. He was a realist about the Congo's growing pains, and full of information. Another friend was Augustin Dokolo, a young man who by his boundless energy had amassed a fortune in the import business during the turbulent days following independence. Augustin later visited us in Washington on a trip to the United States for which Michael had recommended him.

The women who attended the parties were a colorful lot. Wigs were in style there long before they became a fad in the United States, and I shouldn't wonder. It was very difficult to get what you wanted at the hairdresser's. I used to bring my own shampoo and hair spray with me because either the hairdresser would be out of such necessities, or those he had on hand would be of a very poor quality. Congolese wigs, then, had their utilitarian side. Those which the Congolese women wore were fashioned out of coarse hair. They were very heavy, too, especially because of the bulky leather with which they were lined. All of the mistresses of the government ministers owned wigs, and vied with each other in wearing the most spectacular ones.

The wives of Congolese officials were not always in evidence at important parties. Although *purdah* does not exist among the Congolese, their women were under another handicap: they were very poorly educated. Even most of the girls in the Leopoldville schools who were studying to be nurses or technicians were not Congolese. They were often from Nigeria or other West African countries where the policy of the old colonial administrators had been more progressive in that area of education. These girls had come to take advantage of the Congolese facilities when the universities in their own countries became filled.

The parties in Leo were invariably entertaining. Many were held outdoors, and they were fun even though the sharp stones and wet grass were bound to be hard on a lady's gowns and shoes. This wear-and-tear was especially inconvenient because shoes were difficult to buy in Leopoldville, the few that were available being those in odd sizes that had been shipped in left-over lots from New York. Fortunately, I had been told about the shortage and had stocked up before leaving the States.

The memory of one of those parties will remain with me forever. Michael's mother and father were visiting us at the time, which was just before Thanksgiving, 1963. We had been invited to dinner at the home of a prominent Swiss businessman. During the dinner the phone rang and our host went off to answer it. When he returned, looking somber, he went straight over to Michael at the table and whispered something in his ear. I saw Michael start, then excuse himself and leave the room.

Naturally, I was alarmed. I wondered if something had happened to the children. Michael returned after a few minutes, looking very preoccupied, but he resumed his seat and went on eating without saying a word. I was certain that whatever it was did not involve the children, because I knew that he would have told me immediately. But it was evident that he was greatly upset. I slowly finished my dinner, wondering what had happened.

It was only when all of the guests had finished dinner that Michael spoke. "I have some sad news," he said. "President Kennedy has just been assassinated. I called the Marine guard at the Embassy and learned that the report is true."

There seemed to be a low moan all around the table. People, not simply Americans but everyone there, were genuinely affected. The party trailed off, as if nobody had any heart now for conversation. Michael, his parents and I left and drove to the American Embassy. There was a crowd gathered outside the gates, the people just standing there, doing nothing, looking rather stunned. Inside, the silence was oppressive. Everyone, from the ambassador to the most obscure servant, seemed at a loss.

On Sunday a Mass was said for President Kennedy in Leopoldville's big cathedral. It was very impressive. President Kasavubu arrived, escorted by a troop of soldiers. The soldiers lined up inside along the aisles of the cathedral. Every few minutes, at regular intervals, the muted sounds of the Mass would be inundated by a burst of foot-shuffling and rifle-banging as Kasavubu's guards presented arms. Outdoors, cannons boomed in ceaseless salutes.

There were other, gayer moments; and there were times when we were aware of our strong ties to home. One year, as the Fourth of July approached, Betty Kenny (the wife of Michael's immediate boss, George Kenny) and I planned a party for all of the American children living around Leopoldville. We arranged to hold it on the grounds of the American Mission School. Because so many of the items we needed were not available in Leopoldville, we rode the ferry across to Brazzaville and bought them there. We also paid a visit to the tiny PX at the airport. There the colonel was good enough to let us have a supply of chewing gum, candy and other goodies. Our landlord, Maurice Alhadeff, donated soda pop from his soft-drink business, and the small American Air Force contingent stationed at Leo gave us ice cream. Many local people brought us toys which were to be given away as prizes.

On July Fourth the school grounds were crawling with kids. We had created a fish pond, brought in a fortune teller and organized a giant tug-o'-war. The American ambassador appeared and gave a little talk, which the children enjoyed; since all had their mouths full, they couldn't very well interrupt him. It was a delightful day.

One doesn't picture going all the way to the Congo to take part in sports which one associates with home, but it is hardly an exaggeration to say that golf, tennis and water-skiing were as much a part of life in Leopold-ville as in an American suburb. Many diplomats and businessmen belonged to the golf and tennis club founded some years before by the Belgians. In its day the Cercle Royale had been an exclusive club with well-groomed links. During the general instability, however, shabbiness began to crop up. The fairway grass was almost knee-high, the rough had reverted to jungle. But we enjoyed going out on the course when we had free time and hitting a ball around. The tennis courts at the club were in comparatively good condition, and the players showed off to better advantage than the golfers did.

To water-ski, as I mentioned before with swimming, one had to contend with crocodiles (or rumors of them). It was even said that a German diplomat who had drowned while swimming in the Congo had been pulled under by a crocodile. However, the only crocodiles we got close to were a pair named Simone and Antoine in the local zoo. We would pack up a lunch in the morning, drive to the yacht club, where our Portuguese friend Antonio Nogueira kept an outboard motorboat. After piling kids and lunch in the boat, we headed for a sand dune in the Stanley Pool. Sometimes the thick growth of water hyacinths threatened to bog down the boat, but we always managed to plow through to an isolated dune. There we pitched a tent, spread out the picnic, and water-skiied. We always skiied upstream of the dune. The river's current at the Stanley Pool was about ten knots, and just below the pool it boiled up into rapids. We carried a small auxiliary outboard with us in the event the other motor conked out. No one wanted to drift helplessly downstream into that thrashing water!

There was a lovely spot on the river below Leopoldville where we had Sunday picnics with Gina and Jack Tomlinson. He was a cousin of Tommy Tomlinson, our consul-general in Casablanca, and worked for Mobil Oil in the Congo.

One of my most treasured souvenirs of Leopoldville originated in the United States. Before leaving Washington for the Congo, I had spoken to Mrs. Frank Carlucci, whose husband is also in the Foreign Service. It was she who had suggested that I take a clothes dryer with me because of the fly larvae. At the same time she gave me a suggestion which was to prove, if not vital, at least pleasurable. There would be Christmas celebrations, she reminded me; why not take along an artificial Christmas tree?

Mrs. Carlucci's suggestion led, initially, to a lot of headaches. In the rush before leaving for the Congo, I called a number of stores around Washington, looking for the kind of tree I wanted. It had to be a *big* one for the kids. August, I quickly learned, is not the easiest time of the year in which to locate a large artificial Christmas tree. I finally found a store in Maryland which claimed to have what I was looking for. It arrived only five minutes before we were to leave for the Congo. All I could think of at the moment was the stuffed goat! What in the world was I going to do at the last minute with an artificial Christmas tree, six feet tall, when everything else had been crated and shipped?

Fortunately, the tree came packed in two sections. We were able to wedge it into Evans' folding baby bed. But when I at last had a free moment aboard ship and unpacked it to see what the store had sent me, I was dismayed. The tree was hopelessly scrawny. I would be ashamed to set it up for the kids at Christmas.

I refused to give in. Having carried the suggestion that far, I would go a little further. When I arrived in Leo, I wrote to a friend back home and asked her to find and send me a good tree. She came through for us. The tree cost us forty dollars to buy and have shipped to the Congo, but when it arrived in time for our first Christmas there, the pleasure that it gave the children (and Michael and me!) made the whole project worthwhile. I still have the tree—one of our few tangible reminders that the Congo brought us happiness as well as trouble.

16 ★
Stanleyville

Michael's assignment in the Congo was to have an unexpected climax. When we heard the news, we were both quite excited.

We had once more reached that period in an assignment when the time seems to be all downhill until we leave for the United States. Our two years were nearly up. Africa, its strangeness, its dangers, had been grossly overestimated. There had been no sign of savagery. We had lived together in a pleasant house just like (with certain modifications, of course) any other American family. On Michael's vacation we had even boarded a plane and flown to Italy for a month. One approaches Africa with certain misgivings, perhaps, but one's departure is smooth. Soon we would be back in Arizona, or Washington, or some other place, and this vast new

country in central Africa would be for us simply a
friendly, mildly exotic dream.

But fate had a couple of nasty tricks up its sleeve for
us. A curious succession of circumstances started us on
the road to Stanleyville. John Clingerman, the Foreign
Service officer who had met us at the airport on that
long-ago evening when we had arrived in Leopoldville,
played a part in the story's climax. He had been sent
from the Leopoldville Embassy to take charge of the
American Consulate in Stanleyville. Now his tour of duty
in the Congo had expired, and he was returning to the
United States. Michael, with several months remaining of his assignment, was asked to go to Stanleyville to
relieve John Clingerman in July, 1964. A permanent
consul would arrive from Washington at the end of the
summer to relieve Michael.

Both Michael and I looked forward to the Stanleyville post, Michael because for the first time he would
be his own boss, and I because I wanted to see the interior region of the Congo before taking leave of the
country. We had only one reservation. Expecting to be
back in the United States at the beginning of September, we had planned to start the children in school
there. Now we wondered if we would be slightly delayed. As a precaution, we sent Reed, Phelps and Scot
back to my sister in Arizona. Evans would go with us
to Stanleyville.

There was the usual round of farewell parties, the

largest, I must admit, being given this time by the Hoyts themselves. We planned to invite two hundred people. This number seemed to be our capacity, especially in the event of rain, when we could not accommodate many more in our living room and terrace. On the morning of the party Michael gave me one of those shocks to which unsuspecting housewives must grow accustomed. After looking over the list of people we had invited, he confessed that he had asked many more by word of mouth. Our list had swollen to three hundred people.

I worried all day. We had neither the glasses nor the hors d'oeuvres to entertain such a crowd. Fortunately, party lists, like animal populations, have a way of adjusting themselves to the available forage. Some of those who were invited failed to show up, while others remained only a short time. Our provisions held out.

We said our last good-byes, and prepared to leave for Stanleyville. Never could a trip have been so ill-timed as ours. On the fourth anniversary of the Congo's independence, the armed forces of the United Nations pulled out. Few people realized at the time how much the UN had done for the Congo, but one of them was Adlai Stevenson. Speaking of the Congo, Stevenson later said, "The accomplishments of the United Nations are a matter of history. Law and order were maintained, secession was crushed, some advance toward political stability was made, massive economic and technical aid was supplied from all over the world."

Abruptly the whole situation changed for the worse. Largely because France, the USSR and other countries were not willing to continue paying their assessments for the maintenance of a Congo peace force, the UN military force was obliged to leave. The Congo toppled into chaos. The depredations of Communist-armed rebels, which had been contained in the central province of Kwilu, suddenly took on a more prominent and violent tone in the eastern Congo. This disorder laid a serious burden on the Congo's unstable economy. As the revolt began to spread, much of the country's resources had to be marshaled to combat the rebellion. Moishe Tshombe, the central government's old nemesis, was recalled from "exile" to succeed Cyrille Adoula as the Congo's prime minister.

Against this background of events we flew to Stanleyville on the Air Force attaché's Convair, arriving there July 13. For the first time I was a part of the "team." I had been appointed to the Foreign Service staff so that I could serve as Michael's secretary. (For this appointment I was obliged to get a security clearance through the FBI; my clearance came through the day I was evacuated from the city.) As the acting American consul in a critical area, Michael would be receiving and sending classified telegrams and other material, and it was necessary for him to have an American citizen as his secretary. Needless to say, there was a distinct shortage of American women in the area. Joan Allen, an American girl, was already doing secretarial work at the Consulate. There was also a Belgian woman who handled nonconfidential work.

Even before we arrived, many of the Belgian and other European businessmen had sent their wives away from Stan. (Europeans in Africa have a penchant for referring to its cities in abbreviated form: "Stan," "Leo," "E'ville" for Elisabethville, "Jo'burg" for Johannesburg, etc.) Among the people who remained, there was considerable concern for the city's safety. On July 15 Michael assumed his duties as American consul, organizing the Consulate's personnel, while "out there" the rebels were on the move. Nine days later rebel troops captured Kindu, a railroad terminal three hundred miles south of Stanleyville.

Yet I look back today on those weeks before the storm as very pleasant ones. I was occupied throughout the mornings by my secretarial duties at the Consulate, where I worked alongside Michael. I helped Michael make his daily radio contact with the Embassy in Leopoldville. The Consulate building was a spacious home, built some years before by a Belgian doctor for his family. Outside the windows was a broad lawn of thick tropical grass, and beyond it lay a clear view to the wide, swift-flowing river. On the few Sunday afternoons allotted to us there, Michael and I ate our dinner at a fine Italian restaurant located on the banks of that river.

As the wife of the principal officer at the American Consulate, I had certain responsibilities toward the dip-

lomatic community in Stanleyville. Even these responsibilities were pleasant, since most of the entertaining was
informal. Some of the diplomats we mingled with were,
like ourselves, career people: the Belgian consul and
vice-consul, and the Sudanese consul-general and vice-
consul. Others were honorary consuls, men who happened to be in business there and who had been asked
by their foreign ministries to represent them officially to
the local authorities. Peter Rombaud, for instance, was
in the Congo as the chief of a British-American tobacco
company, the Companie Congolese du Tabac, but he
also served as the honorary British vice-consul. There
were also honorary Greek and Cypriot consuls. Because
most of the wives of both the diplomats and the businessmen had already left Stanleyville, I found that most
of my "entertaining" was restricted to stag lunches.

The servant problem was all but solved for me. Instead of hunting for a "nanny," I found ready-made
baby-sitters for Evans in two "Pax boys" who were working at the University of Stanleyville. They were American boys who were conscientious objectors; when they
had refused to enter military service in the United
States, they had taken the alternative of serving their
time doing useful work overseas. They made excellent
baby-sitters. Evans got along fine with them, and I paid
them off in such commodities as vanilla or Tang, a powdered orange juice. On occasion I used to hire a young
woman attached to the missionary establishment. Her
name was Phyllis Rine. At the horrible climax of the

Congo rescue operation, two Americans were killed in Stanleyville by rebel machine-gunners. One was Dr. Paul Carlson. The other was Phyllis Rine.

The cook at the Consulate was a very old and deaf African, Tata Paul. In the evenings he would cook our dinners, then leave immediately afterward because he liked to spend as much time as possible with his family, but in that troubled atmosphere, did not like to be on the roads after dark. When the rebels captured Stanleyville, Tata Paul loyally stayed on at the Consulate to help his American friends. Riding home on his bicycle after work one day he was shot and killed by the Simbas.

In those long afternoons before the disaster, when I was free of my Consulate duties, Evans and I leisurely walked down the broad avenues of Stanleyville. It was pleasant to take in the spectacle of the city and relish the sense of isolation from the outside world. There were sights that I was to recall with intense clarity during the succeeding months. One of them was the zoo, with its scrawny animals, near Tshopo Falls. (When the rebels later controlled the city, they threw many of their victims, sewn in bags, over these falls. And on another occasion the Simba leaders threatened to cage Michael and his colleagues in the zoo and exhibit them to the populace.) Another sight that haunted me afterward was the big square in the center of Stanleyville. It had been renamed "Lumumba Square" in honor of the slain leftist leader. Here his admirers had erected a large monument lined with white bathroom tiles. Inserted in the monument, behind a pane of glass, was a photograph in color of Lumumba, his long thin face ornamented with a goatee, his right arm raised, his left resting on a globe. Beneath the photograph were these words:

> Here is the monument of the Liberator of the Congo, Premier Patrice Emery Lumumba, Hero of Independence and of unity, assassinated 18 January, 1961, in Katanga.

But perhaps the memory from those days that will stay longest with me was that of our visit to François Aradjabu, the provincial president. It was a courtesy call, which I, as the wife of the new American consul, was obliged to pay to the wife of the highest-ranking local dignitary. Aradjabu lived in the sumptuous Governor's Residence, which was almost as large as the mansion in which Kasavubu lived at Leopoldville. It had a wide view of the great river. Michael came with me to translate, and by a stroke of good fortune we decided to bring Evans with us.

When we arrived we were ushered into the big living room, where we were greeted by Aradjabu's wife. The room was furnished with two rows of armchairs. One chair, in the most prominent place, was embroidered with a large golden *P*, which stood for President. Evans immediately went and sat down in the big chair (what child wouldn't?). For a moment I was wondering whether or not we should have brought him.

Presently Aradjabu entered the room. He went around and shook hands gravely with each of us, leaving Evans until last. Evans, of course, had to stand to shake hands with the imposing stranger, and Aradjabu, who had eight children of his own and probably considerable experience in handling situations of this kind, gently shoved Evans aside and took his proper seat. Evans was a little miffed, but he came over and sat down next to me, and the whole affair went off very well. In fact, Evans gave us all something to talk about. Michael and I talked with Aradjabu and his wife for some time about children, and everyone felt at ease. Later, when I learned that this gentle Congolese official had been executed following the rebellion, I felt very bad.

It was the last pleasant memory I retain of Stanleyville. In a few days the rebels were at the city's gates. There was the last-minute flurry of packing, saying good-bye to Michael, then flying to Leopoldville with Evans. There was Michael's voice on the radio, the fragmentary news as the rebels overran the city—and then silence. Michael's life hung on the hate-driven, drug-twisted wills of unknown men.

17.

The Long Wait Begins

The next ten days in Leopoldville were a nightmare for me, a foretaste of the frustrating months ahead. We had landed there after a four-hour flight from Stanleyville. Several planes left the besieged city after ours, one of them carrying the two USIS men and the girl tourists, but the two communications men, Ernie Houle and Donald Parkes, had been unable to get through to the airport as planned. They joined Michael, David Grinwis and James Stauffer at the Consulate.

Though Stanleyville had been overrun by the rebels, I found reason to be hopeful when Michael's voice continued to come through to Leopoldville over the radio. Every day I went either to the Embassy or to the home of one of the military attachés, where I listened anxiously for Michael's call on the radio. Yet even at those moments when I was elated simply to know that

Michael was out there some place and could talk to us, I was nagged by the thought which was to torture me increasingly as the days went by. Michael was not *really* free to talk to us, and we were powerless to help him.

This became more obvious every day. The Consulate staff was at the mercy of the Simbas. Every message that Michael sent to Leopoldville by radio or telegram during those first few days reflected his predicament. He reported that the Consulate was attacked by the rebels the day after I left. Michael and his staff crowded into the Consulate vault. The Simbas swept into the building, smashing doors and windows, firing indiscriminately around them. The staff heard them shouting and banging as they tried to breach the vault's heavy door. They poured bullets into its steel plate. ("We thought they'd started shooting at it with a cannon," Michael said later. "The noise was magnified a hundred times in the vault.") And then, as abruptly as they had come, the rebels faded away. Michael and the others were free to come out of the vault.

The situation remained desperate. After the first violent attack by the Simbas, who in their wild excitement certainly would have slaughtered whatever foreigners they had come across in the Consulate, Michael and his staff decided to remain in the open and try to carry out their work. This consisted of the hopeless task that had been assigned them: to remain in Stanleyville as long as possible and protect American lives and property. In the face of the Simbas' outrageous behavior, the whole world began very slowly to realize that nothing short of armed might could alter the grim drama that was taking place in Stanleyville. The rebels were murdering thousands of Africans, in both the city and the surrounding countryside. News of the slaughter emerged only sporadically. It was the more frightening because we knew so little of what was really going on.

I was driven nearly frantic by this hunger for news. I pleaded for information at the Embassy, but I could get little satisfaction. Either the people there knew little more than I did, or they were afraid to tell me how serious the situation really was.

On August 7, three days after I arrived, I learned that plans were being contemplated to rescue Michael and the others. One serious difficulty was that there seemed to be no way of sending a confidential message to Michael. Every broadcast, it was feared, might be monitored by the rebels or by groups friendly to them. Any messages that might enflame them to new outrages had to be avoided. The men at the Embassy in Leo tried to get information by devious methods. At this time they wanted to know whether all the Americans would be within reach of the rescuers.

"What do you do for amusement up there?" Monty Stearns, the Embassy's political officer, asked Michael in an attempt to gather last-minute information.

"We play bridge," Michael answered.

"All of you?"

"We have to contact our kibitzer by telephone."

This reply alerted the people in Leo that Ernie Houle was still cut off from the others in his downtown apartment.

In the end, Michael asked the Embassy not to consider any further rescue operation. There were too many armed Simbas in the vicinity of the Consulate. Even if the attempt succeeded, Ernie, the American missionaries and anyone else left behind would face almost certain death.

Another message came from Michael on August 10. The Consulate staff had been under constant harassment from roving bands of undisciplined Simbas. In an effort to protect lives and property from these people, Michael went with members of "third country" consulates and representatives of the local business community to see the rebel commander, General Nicolas Olenga. The meeting had progressed in a bizarre but orderly fashion until Olenga spotted Michael and learned that he was the American consul. Apparently he had recently been indoctrinated in anti-Americanism by his Chinese Communist supporters. He ordered Michael and the other Americans to be sent home from Stanleyville on the first available plane. Michael returned to the Consulate to contact us; it proved to be the last time we heard his voice for months:

"We have been ordered by the authorities to be evacuated but I do not recommend that any special transportation arrangements be made."

The last phrase of the message canceled the hope that had been stirred by its opening. Michael was telling the Embassy that he was *persona non grata,* but that any attempt to send a plane to evacuate him and the staff would be dangerous. He had been ordered to leave by General Olenga, but there was no means of evacuating him.

Only the presence of little Evans, whose constant demands diverted me occasionally from the horror in Stanleyville, kept me from breaking down. I persisted in my demands that I be told *everything.* But the truth was, I am afraid, that there was little to tell me. Embassy and State Department opinion was divided on the question of what could be done. Some officials wanted to take stronger action before the rebels consolidated their position. Others, considering international complications and the possible danger to the staff, advised caution. So many of my friends sustained me during those days. They sympathized, they comforted me, but they were unanimous in their opinion that I could do nothing, either for Michael or myself, in Leopoldville.

"You're killing yourself here," Jack Tomlinson told me. "Take Evans and get out of this place. Go home."

I held on. I couldn't help but feel that leaving now would be to desert Michael. It was irrational, but I had very few rational thoughts during the early days of my ordeal. Then a message came through from Michael: "Tell my number one to go to Jerome."

I knew instantly, of course, what he meant. Michael wanted me to go back to Jerome, Arizona, where my sister and her husband had a summer home. But the message puzzled the Embassy staff. They were sure that the words conveyed something else. Michael, they reasoned, was telling them to go to Jerome for certain information. But Jerome who? Was it Jerome Anany, a former minister of defense in the central government. They went to him, but he was as puzzled as they. In different circumstances it would have been uproariously funny. But I wasn't laughing.

The message from Michael had jolted me from my own confusion, and I saw that my only course was to take Evans and rejoin the rest of the children in Arizona. In Leo, I was a pest to the Embassy people and a menace to myself. There were no further messages from Stanleyville. The Consulate had been completely cut off from the outside world. Michael's radio had gone dead. On August 15 I completed my arrangements to leave. Taking with me only the single suitcase I had carried out of Stanleyville, I boarded a plane with Evans for Rome.

The trip home was something of a revelation to me. Isolated in the Congo, I had come to look on the whole affair as a personal catastrophe. It was *my* husband who was in peril; therefore it was *my* worry. Then I discovered that the incident was not simply personal or local; it was an international story. The news had appeared in the *New York Times, Le Figaro, Informacion* and the *Daily Express*. When I stopped to visit relatives in Evansville, Indiana, I discovered Michael's picture in the local paper (an old college snapshot, with Michael looking very young and needing a haircut; Evans thought it was a "lousy" picture). When I went on to Chicago to catch the plane to Tucson, I was met at the airport by a photographer from the Chicago *Tribune*. Later, TWA gave me VIP treatment, putting me aboard the plane ahead of the other passengers. Somehow it was all very unnerving. Evans was already upset and sleeping badly, asking for his daddy. I had learned in Evansville that an Arizona newspaper had already "interviewed" the other children in Jerome; their picture had appeared in the paper, the three of them trying to cuddle their puppy "Chongo" for the insistent photographer. I was afraid of what effect the building tension might have on them.

The sight of Reed, Phelps and Scot gave me a temporary lift. With Michael constantly in my thoughts during the preceding weeks, I hadn't realized how much I missed them. The children were positively blooming in the Arizona mountains. They had all been to the dentist to have their teeth fixed, Reed was in the open air all day, trying to catch things like fish and snakes, and Phelps and Scot were excited by the art lessons they had been taking from a local painter. The children loved Arizona, and had felt quite at home there in the mountains with my sister Charlotte and her husband, Branson Smith. For a few happy moments Africa seemed nearly as remote as it had when I was a girl.

Yet once I was alone, it all flooded back on me. To know that Michael was in danger was bad enough. The uncertainty was a torture. In my restlessness I reached for any possible straw. Twice in those early days I actually lifted the telephone and placed a call to the American Consulate in Stanleyville. That was a mistake. The first time the operator told me she would keep on trying, but eventually there was something grim and final about her routine announcement: "That line is out of order."

I turned to the mails. Nearly every day I wrote to Michael. I intended them to be long, chatty letters, full of news about the children and the placid rhythm of our days in Jerome. But each letter somehow disintegrated into a jumble—an old association would rip my mind from Jerome and send it thousands of miles to I knew not what terrible place where Michael was surrounded by enemies. Then the gossip was forgotten in my plea: *"Please* come home!" I addressed each letter to a different place, hoping that one, at least, would find its way through to Michael. Stanleyville . . . Leopoldville . . . Belgian businessmen in Brussels . . . the International Red Cross in Geneva . . . the American Embassy in Bujumbura, Burundi. I sent them off to Michael, knowing that they probably would never reach him in Stanleyville. None of them did. Writing to a loved one under those circumstances was like shouting down an ancient well. Only the sound of my own voice, strained and unfamiliar, came back to me.

My only other release was a regular telephone call to the State Department in Washington. As soon as I arrived in Jerome, I began calling there, asking for news. The people I talked to were very kind, but they had nothing to tell me. I wanted to rush off to Washington immediately, to pound on doors, to make myself heard so that *somebody* would take action and bring Michael home to me. But here Branson Smith, my brother-in-law, stepped in. He said that the idea of going to Washington was a good one, and that eventually I must go and talk to the people there. But this, he said, wasn't the time to go. I must collect myself, think out in advance what I would tell them, what information I had that might help them in their struggle to free Michael. When I got there I should be able to help, not simply to complain. Later Branson told me that I was so distraught he feared I would do more harm than good in Washington. Reluctantly, I put off my trip.

The summer was drawing to an end. For the children's sake I was happy that we had been able to spend the first of those agonizing months in the isolation of Jerome. At the turn of the century Jerome had been a copper-mining town. With the exhaustion of the supply of copper, Jerome had reverted to obscurity. A few artists had come to settle, then other people looking for secluded summer homes in the cool mountains. A small tourist business has sprung up, taking advantage of the abandoned mines and the legends that flourish around ghost towns. Curios were sold. Here, in the absence of the steady stream of news that assaults our eyes and ears in the city, we could follow the sensible plan proposed by Branson. When Stanleyville fell, the children had read about it in the newspapers and heard about it on television. I had been "evacuated," their father had remained in a battle-torn city where the bullets whistled around him. The children didn't know what to make of it all. It was then that Branson decided to "censor" what they read and heard. If the news was to be bad, he wanted them to hear it from those who loved them and were aware of their pain. Incomplete or distorted news reports were also to be guarded against. After I reached Jerome we continued to follow this plan.

But now the time had come for us to move to Tucson, where Branson taught school. This would throw the children back into the environment of news and chatter from which we had tried to shield them. For the smaller children the change would not be so unsettling. But Reed was now thirteen years old. One cannot hope to fool a boy like that for very long. Here Branson again came up with the solution. There was a private school outside the city where Reed could board during the week, but it was close enough so that he could be with us on weekends. In that school he would find the isolation we wanted for him.

Again I contacted the State Department in Washington. The people there could tell me nothing. Be patient, they said, we're doing everything we can. But short of Michael's release, nothing could satisfy me.

18 ★
Hope Fades

In Stanleyville, Michael's life was constantly in jeopardy. Once he and the other Americans had emerged from the Consulate vault, they were defenseless. Any of the roving bands of Simbas, their old uniforms trimmed with the fur of lions and monkeys, could enter the Consulate and take whatever vengeance on them that hate or drugs might suggest. It was not until his first interview with General Olenga (when he had been declared *persona non grata*) that Michael discovered the source of this intense hatred of the Americans. Olenga, who wore a Vandyke beard and a mustache, was an erratic man who fluctuated between gallantry and cruelty. On this occasion he worked himself into a frenzy, spouting the propaganda he had picked up from the Communist agents.

"You Americans are interfering in the affairs of the

Congo," he roared. "They are the cause of our trouble. They have killed our soldiers. They are killing our women and children. I should know—I have captured a hundred and eight American soldiers!"

When Michael tried to tell him that there were no American troops fighting in the Congo, Olenga ignored him. Michael's attempts to convince him that American lives and property in Stanleyville must be protected were treated in the same manner. In place of a reply, a group of young officers standing behind Olenga broke into an unnerving chant: "Etats Unis d'Amerique . . . Etats Unis d'Amerique . . . Etats Unis d'Amerique!"

The Americans were forced to fend for themselves in this hostile city. On August 7 a band of Simbas arrived at the Consulate to confiscate the American cars. When Michael could not find the keys to one of the cars, the Simbas threatened to torture, kill and then eat the Americans.

One Simba pointed his rifle at Michael's chest. "I can kill you," he said.

"Yes," Michael nodded. "But why would I risk death to save the car?"

The puzzled Simba wavered, then swung his rifle at Michael's head and walked away.

On August 11 Ernie Houle made his way back to the Consulate from the downtown apartment where he had been trapped. It was a bad day for the Consulate staff. A Simba major appeared and began boasting to the Americans of his immunity to bullets. He laid the rifle at Michael's feet and told him to pick it up and shoot him. When Michael refused, the major said that it proved his immunity. The Simbas then began beating Michael and the others with their rifle butts, and jabbing at them with their bayonets. Several of the Americans were bleeding.

The major ordered Michael to open the door to the vault, which had been jammed. (Michael and the others had been able to enter it through a hole they had cut in the ceiling.) Michael worked desperately with a hammer and chisel to open the door, while the Simbas prodded him with their rifle butts and threatened him with death. One of them stamped on his hand. Finally Michael managed to open the vault for the Simbas to inspect; luckily they never noticed the hole in the ceiling. Meanwhile, other Simbas had pulled down the American flag from the Consulate pole and ordered the staff to chew on it. Houle, Stauffer, Grinwis and Parkes, with the excited Simbas standing menacingly over them, chewed on the heavy cloth.

The major then herded Michael and the others into a truck and drove them to General Olenga's headquarters. Dried fish heads, which littered the back of the truck, were stuffed into their mouths. When they arrived at headquarters, a wild-eyed mob of Simbas surrounded the truck. "*Mateke!*" they screamed at the Americans. "Dead Flesh!" They began to beat them, clamoring for their immediate execution. Abruptly, another officer arrived and pulled the Americans to safety. Later General Olenga appeared and apologized to Michael, saying he did not want "to break diplomatic relations with the United States." He also said that he had changed his mind about evacuating the Consulate staff.

Yet each day brought its new harassment and its new terrors. Michael and the staff lived under the hourly threat of death. Simbas moved into the Consulate, demanding food and beer. One day they took the Americans to the air terminal and, along with six unfortunate Congolese and an American missionary, locked them in the women's toilet. There was not even enough room for them to squat in the filthy, airless hole. The prisoners stood there for three days, alternately threatened or beaten by their captors.

Then, just as abruptly, the Americans were moved to the Sabena Guest House, across from the terminal. There, for four weeks, they lived in relative comfort. The food was edible, and a Belgian physician, Dr. Alexander Barlovatz, sent in books to them. But the threat was always around them. The doctor told of witnessing the ritual murders of hundreds of Congolese in Lumumba Square. Intellectuals, captured Congolese army officers and members of the previous administration were cut down by the screaming Simbas. After one former official was killed in the square, the doctor said he saw the crowd dismember his body and eat his liver. The square through which Evans and I used to wander so peacefully was now soaked with blood.

Occasionally, wounded rebel soldiers on their way to

the nearby hospital stopped outside the Guest House to shriek threats at the Americans. They claimed that their wounds had been inflicted by American troops. Once a young Simba entered the room where Michael and the others were held and began beating them savagely, cutting both Parkes and the missionary, Chuck Davis, on the head. Ernie Houle, who was fifty-three years old, pretended to faint. At this, the Simba grew quite alarmed, apologized hastily and ran out. In a few minutes he returned, carrying the prisoners' supper.

Time and again, Michael and the others encountered this eccentric behavior in their captors. At one moment they would be stripped and made to crawl across the floor on their hands and knees while the Simbas drew blood with their rifle butts and bayonets. The next moment the Simbas would relent, offer their apologies and try to relieve their victims' discomfort. Just as variable were the orders from above. After four weeks in the Guest House the Americans were removed to the city prison, where they slept on boards in damp cells, wearing only their shorts and jerseys, their requests for blankets having been denied. Then they were returned to the Guest House, then moved into the Congo Palace, the finest hotel in Stanleyville. Michael always made it his practice to remain on the best possible terms with their guards, sharing his food and cigarettes with these youngsters, who often appeared to be half-starved.

Once the Americans were pushed into a school bus and driven through the streets of the city. There they were exposed to the taunts and blows of the crowds. The driver told Michael that they were being taken to Lumumba Square. That, as everyone knew, was the end of the road. The driver thought it a great joke when he finally deposited them safely back at the hotel.

And yet there were times when Michael was treated with considerable respect by the rebel officers. They spoke vaguely to him of "diplomatic negotiations." For a while it seemed that the efforts of the British and Belgian consuls, who were still free to move around Stanleyville, might persuade the rebels to abide by civilized codes in dealing with their prisoners. But the rebels refused to release them, and forced Michael to send messages, dictated by themselves, to the American Embassy in Leopoldville.

Once more the Americans were taken to the city prison, where they remained for almost six weeks. Every indication of normal diplomatic activity disappeared. The rebel leaders began to lock up all the Americans and Belgians they could find. Michael and his staff were joined in the city prison by Baron Patrick Nothomb, the Belgian consul, and his vice-consul, Paul Duque. The new prisoners also included the two American conscientious objectors who had done some baby-sitting for us before the city's fall.

The pressure on the prisoners became almost unbearable. Some of the men had already written farewell notes to their families. Michael, in a letter to me which he had little hope of sending out of Stanleyville and which I did not see until the ordeal had ended, wrote these words: "Jo, all through these times I have been thinking constantly of you and my sole wish has been that I would survive to see you and the children. I have looked death in the face many times since seeing you and each time I have fought to stay alive in order that you would not have the pain of my death. I hope that the news you have been getting does not reflect the very real danger to our lives that we have been under."

In Tucson, I craved news—any news—of Michael's condition. It was almost impossible to find. After the brief flurry of stories that had appeared in the newspapers at the time of Stanleyville's fall, the subject seemed to fade from people's minds. One reason for this, of course, was the progress of the presidential campaign. Both candidates were, in a sense, "local boys," Lyndon Johnson coming from the southwestern state of Texas, and Barry Goldwater from Arizona itself. The local papers were full of campaign news. Each day we read the papers, or went over to a neighbor's house to watch the news programs on television, hoping to come across some small item from the Congo. We were seldom rewarded. The Congo seemed as remote as it had in the days of H. M. Stanley.

This was effectively brought home to us by an experience that Branson Smith had in school. During the lunch period one day, Branson was sitting in the teachers' lounge, talking with some of his colleagues about current affairs. Someone mentioned the Congo.

"Do you know that right now there are five American State Department people being held hostage in the Congo?" Branson asked them.

There were fifteen other teachers in the room. Two seemed vaguely aware of some sort of a dispute. The rest knew nothing about it. Several of them refused to believe Branson's account, one of them even accusing Branson of being "a Goldwater fanatic" who was trying to discredit the Johnson administration.

Stories such as this combined to frustrate me even further. There was no aroused public opinion to protest this almost unprecedented affront to the United States and its official representatives abroad. The tiny items that did appear occasionally in the newspapers were discouraging. On September 4 there was a story quoting General Olenga that he was holding all white men, women and children in the northeast Congo as hostages against government air raids. A later report placed the number of these hostages at 525, including the five American State Department people. On September 10 it was announced that in response to the pleas of Congo President Joseph Kasavubu, the Organization of African Unity would try to restore order in the troubled country. Yet nothing came of it. Other reports said the Republic of the Congo at Brazzaville (the old French Congo) had permitted the rebels to establish a headquarters and a training camp on their territory. Arms and other supplies were being sent to the rebels from Communist China, Egypt, Algeria and several Eastern European countries. Other African nations rejected Kasavubu's calls for help. It began to appear that other countries were encouraging notions of grandeur among the rebels. There was something sinister lurking beneath the absurd boasts made by the rebels, including that of "President" Christophe Gbenye after the fall of Stanleyville.

"We will push on to Leopoldville," he had said, "then to Brussels, and then to New York. Someday the world will be ours!"

I grasped at every shred of credible information. At times I felt my best sources were the friends we had made in Leopoldville. Some of them kindly kept in touch with me. One American businessman wrote to me from Brussels that he had heard the food situation "had deteriorated for Europeans in Stan." He went on to say that "Mike and four other Americans were roughed up and jailed when the rebels first took over. Then they were released from jail, and all five placed under heavy guard at the old Sabena Guest House, all five in one room." And he added, "The Belgian consul in Stan is being accorded diplomatic courtesies and is looking after all Europeans, regardless of nationality. Unfortunately he cannot do anything for the Americans, who were singled out for harsh treatment. I am strongly advised against attempting to make any contact with Mike or sending him a message, as it may jeopardize his already precarious position."

In my frantic attempts to goad *somebody* into positive action, I thought of appealing to public opinion through the newspapers, or contacting any of a number of Congressmen. Before going ahead with this plan, however, I called the State Department. Through Lew Hoffaker, who had worked with Michael in the Congo and who had survived a precarious moment or two himself while serving as consul in Elisabethville during the Tshombe secession, the State Department advised me against this course.

"I cannot see how any such measures will advance Mike's cause," Lew wrote to me late in September. "In fact, I can see how public notice of his plight might even increase the intransigence and the bargaining price of the rebels. However, if you would feel better by contacting members of Congress, that of course is your own decision to make."

I knew he was right, and I dropped the plan. However, he insisted that if I had questions or felt uneasy, I call anyone working on the Congo, and he supplied me with the office and home numbers of all concerned. "I do not know when I have seen such a concerted and imaginative effort focused on a project as is now under way on Mike's behalf," Lew wrote. I was grateful for the letter.

Now, almost every day, I called the State Department. But the information they could give me was still pitifully meager. Some of it, as we learned later, was inaccurate. On September 25 a Red Cross plane flew into Stanleyville, and my hopes went up. But they came to earth just as quickly. The rebel officials refused to permit the Red Cross to evacuate anyone from the city. And Michael, wisely judging that the letter he had been writing to me over a long period might inflame the rebel officers who would surely look it over before sending it on, decided against posting it.

Then, on October 1, I received a phone call from Lew Hoffaker.

"I wanted you to know this before the press gets hold of it," he told me. "We've intercepted a message from a Colonel Opepe in Stanleyville to rebel leaders. He's asking permission to kill the American hostages."

19 ★
Washington

I began to come apart at the seams. Weeks of tension had broken down my resistance, and this latest announcement almost drove me wild. The State Department had shown its good faith by preparing me for what they felt might be the report of Michael's death. But it wasn't enough. I felt the whole situation had distintegrated into a monstrous charade, with an unstable and disorganized bandit regime exposing the United States to ridicule. I made up my mind to go to Washington.

Branson and Charlotte supported my decision. They knew that I had explored so many avenues that by then I was able to distinguish between those that led nowhere and those that might be helpful. I was in no mood to remain a passive onlooker. I suspected that I had not been told everything I ought to have known about Michael's plight, and that only by going to highly placed people in Washington could I get the information to which I, as Michael's wife, believed I was entitled. What confirmed my decision to go was that earlier I had been invited there by G. Mennen "Soapy" Williams, the former Governor of Michigan and the then Assistant Secretary of State for African Affairs. I called the State Department and said that I was ready to accept Governor Williams' invitation. The next day, October 2, almost two months after I had last seen Michael, I boarded a plane for Washington.

I arrived on a Thursday evening. At the terminal, quite by accident, I met Ed Gullion, the former ambassador in Leopoldville, who had come down from Tufts College to talk with State Department officials about Michael and the Congo problem. Then I went to the home of Lew and Connie Hoffaker. Though Governor Williams graciously had invited me to stay with his family in Washington, I accepted the Hoffakers' invitation because we had known them in Leopoldville, where they had been our neighbors and where our children had played together. I reasoned that now it would be easier to stay with old friends.

"Whom do you want to see?" Lew asked me.

"I'll start at the top and work down," I said.

And Lew made the necessary appointments for me. I arrived at the State Department early Friday morning. There I discovered that a large and busy "Task Force" had been assembled to attempt to restore order in the Congo and to devise means for rescuing Michael and the other Americans there. The group was headed by Ambassador Joseph Palmer, the Director-General of the Foreign Service. He had lived day and night with the problem since Stanleyville fell on August 4, and he was directly responsible to Governor Williams. Around him I discovered many old friends, equally concerned for Michael's safety. There was Jim O'Sullivan, formerly the ambassador's deputy in Leopoldville; Bill Schaufele, Michael's colleague at the Consulate in Casablanca and now recently returned from the Consulate at Bukavo in the Congo to serve as the Congo desk officer; and John Clingerman, Michael's predecessor as consul in Stanleyville. There for the first time I met Walker Diamante, whom I had called many times from Arizona and whom I would be in touch with even more closely in the future. George Ball and former Governor Averell Harriman of New York, then the number two and three men in the State Department, were in constant and detailed contact with Congo developments.

Because of a queer twist of fate, I was able to tour the highly secret Operations Center. Only persons with the highest security clearance are allowed to enter the room. I had applied for that when I became Michael's secretary in Stanleyville, such clearance supposedly being necessary to handle top-secret documents. As I mentioned before, this clearance had arrived from Washington on the day Evans and I were evacuated from Stanleyville. Now I was able to put it to use.

It was in the Operations Center that one of the few

"light" moments of my visit to Washington occurred. In the middle of a conversation about something else, Bill Schaufele broke in. "What the hell have you done to your hair, Jo?" he asked.

"I had it frosted just before I left Tucson," I told him. "I figured I needed *something* to cheer me up."

The other men who had been standing around began to laugh. It turned out that all those who had known me before had been shocked at my appearance, assuming that the ordeal had turned my hair gray. Until then no one had dared to mention it.

It was while I was in the Operations Center that a call came from the office of Arizona Congressman Morris Udall. Udall also has an interest in a Tucson newspaper. Apparently, a reporter, checking the passenger list at the airport, noticed that I had boarded a plane for Washington. Udall's office assumed that I had flown there because of an imminent news break. Either Michael had been released by the rebels, or he had been killed. The Congressman wanted to know.

"Mrs. Hoyt is here now," Walker Diamante, who had taken the call, told Udall's assistant. "Why don't you ask her?"

Walker handed the phone to me. I assured the caller that neither conjecture was true. There was no change in the situation. However, I asked him not to publish the news that I was in Washington, because publicity at that point might jeopardize the negotiations for Michael's release. I promised that as soon as there was anything to report I would notify the Tucson paper. Udall's assistant agreed to drop the story.

Through Lew Hoffaker, I made appointments to see Governor Williams, his deputy, Wayne Fredericks, and Secretary of State Dean Rusk. Both Governor Williams, just back from a trip abroad, and Wayne Fredericks were very helpful, answering my questions and filling me in on details of Michael's imprisonment that I had not yet heard.

My appointment with Secretary Rusk, scheduled for Saturday morning, had been postponed until Monday because of the arrival in Washington of a touring chief of state. My friends did all they could to take my mind off my troubles over the weekend. Connie Hoffaker took me shopping so that I could buy presents for the children. The Schaufeles invited me for cocktails, the Sullivans asked me to dinner. I'm afraid that I wasn't very good company. Afterward I realized that the experience must have been as painful for my friends as it was for me, and I was grateful for their constant sympathy.

On Monday morning Walker Diamante escorted me into the spacious but simply decorated office of Secretary Rusk on the seventh floor of the State Department Building. I was now face to face with the man who directed thousands of men and women in the business of carrying out the foreign policy of the United States. This was the Cabinet officer who by law and tradition is the President's principal adviser on the ultimate decisions in the field of foreign policy and his principal agent in carrying out those decisions. And yet he spent twenty-five minutes talking to me and, more importantly, listening to me recite my troubles.

Contrary to the impression given by many of his pictures, Dean Rusk is a large man, but he is a very gentle man, too. The eyes that looked back at me from his round, freckled face were friendly and understanding. He spoke softly, assuring me of his concern for Michael and outlining much of what was being done to bring the Americans out of Stanleyville. He spoke to me very candidly.

"Your husband and the others are in real danger," he said. "We have no certain solution in sight. We hope for an easy evacuation when and if the Red Cross plane can go back into Stanleyville. But even if some people can be evacuated on that plane, we have no assurance that Mr. Hoyt and his staff will be allowed to leave."

The Secretary's voice took on a firmness I hadn't heard before. "We will use every means at our disposal to get your husband out of Stanleyville," he said.

If I had expected to hear a glibly reassuring monologue, I was agreeably surprised. The Secretary sat back and let me unburden myself. I told him of my apprehensions that important information had been withheld from me. I could, I felt sure, be of more help to myself and to the State Department if I had some idea of what was going on. At this point I suggested the names of people in Leopoldville's business community with whom

Michael had dealt, people who presumably maintained contact with their associates in Stanleyville. The Secretary asked Walker Diamante to add those names to the list already compiled by the Congo Task Force. Then his face softened.

"How are the children taking this, Mrs. Hoyt?" he asked.

"Well, it's hard on them," I told him. "Little Evans wants to know why his daddy hasn't come home. When a four-year-old asks a question like that, it's time his daddy *did* come home!"

As I rose to leave, the Secretary again assured me that everything possible was being done to bring Michael safely home. "I can't reveal *all* the measures we're taking at this time," he said. "One false step could touch off a blood bath. One unfortunate item in the press could stir up those people. But I promise you that if it becomes necessary to undertake any moves that might involve a risk for your husband, we will let you know ahead of time."

He instructed Walker Diamante to keep in daily contact with me. Every scrap of information that might keep me up with the true situation was to be passed on to me. "And if you get depressed and you think it would make you feel better"—the Secretary smiled— "don't be afraid to pick up the telephone and call me. I'll talk to you at any time."

I was grateful for the interview. I felt that in my talk with Dean Rusk, as in all my other contacts at the

State Department on this visit, I had been treated seriously. The people I had talked to had been candid and genuinely sympathetic. I was now convinced of their concern and their determination to bring Michael home. Yet as I flew back to Arizona, I realized that if *my* pain had been somewhat relieved, Michael's plight remained absolutely unaltered.

20 ★
Massacre!

Back in Tucson, Charlotte, Branson and the children sustained me. Evans was a blessing. He seemed to absorb my moods, so that when things were very bad and I became cranky and depressed, he behaved identically. He was naughty, and so had to be disciplined or loved. For those few minutes, then, I would be distracted from the inner pain that was always with me.

Away from me, Evans was as dignified and grave as a little old man. In kindergarten his teacher told the class that Evans' father was being held a prisoner by a bunch of bad men. Evans shook his head impatiently. "They're not bad," he told the teacher. "They're just misguided."

Charlotte and Branson generously turned over their home to us, while they moved into a nearby apartment. Reed, of course, was away at school during the week, but he showed the strain of the ordeal when he came home on weekends. I wanted him to feel secure.

"If you hear anything while you're at school," I told him, "and you are worried about it, call me and ask. If I don't know anything, I'll call the State Department and find out."

It was comforting to have Reed with us on weekends, but Charlotte and Branson kept watch on me during the week. On days when I had received especially discouraging news, Branson used any means at hand to snap me out of my despondency, even making cutting remarks that would force me to vent my frustration in an outburst of anger.

Charlotte came to visit every day. She wanted to get me out of the house as much as possible, but I let nothing interfere with my daily call from Walker Diamante. Usually his call came late in the day, after all the reports had come in to Washington. But if the phone rang in the morning, and the operator announced that I had a call from Washington, I trembled all over. I knew then that the news was of more than routine interest, and that it was likely to be unsettling. Through it all, Walker remained patient and understanding. He never seemed to be in a hurry to hang up, and I am sure that there were many times when he wished himself rid of me. The more frantic, the more demanding, I became, the greater his sympathy. Charlotte told me later that she was unable to remain in the house while I was talking to Walker. The sound of my voice, frightened or pleading,

made her break into tears and she would walk outside
and wait until I had finished. I owe a great deal, perhaps even my sanity, to Walker Diamante.

He had very little good news to report to me. Every
avenue the State Department explored seemed to prove
at last a blind alley. In fact, matters were growing
worse. Later in October the rebels arrested Dr. Paul
Carlson, an American missionary, and announced that
he would be tried as an "American officer." Carlson,
who had worked hard among the Congolese, relieving
their sufferings, was pushed into the city prison with
Michael and the other members of the Consulate staff.
We also learned that all the Americans and Belgians in
the area had been rounded up as "hostages" against the
counteroffensive being mounted by the central government.

There were certain signs now that this government,
under President Kasavubu and Prime Minister Tshombe,
had weathered the storm and was striking back. There
was, for instance, this advertisement in a South African
newspaper:

> Any fit young man looking for employment with a dif-
> ference at a salary well in excess of 100 pounds per
> month should telephone 838-5202/3 during business
> hours. Employment initially offered for 6 months. Im-
> mediate start.

The "fit young men" who presented themselves in answer to these ads found that their employer was to be

the Congolese government, and they were to serve as mercenaries in the drive to recapture Stanleyville. Meanwhile the rebels continued to breathe defiance. "President" Christophe Gbenye, in his Stanleyville newspaper *Le Martyr*, was quoted as threatening his hostages. "We will make fetishes out of the hearts of Americans and Belgians," he said, "and we will dress ourselves in their skins."

The government troops continued to advance on Stanleyville. On November 18 Michael and his staff, Dr. Carlson and the two young American conscientious objectors, Jon Snyder and Gene Bergman, were dragged out of the prison and loaded into a couple of jeeps. When they found themselves being taken to the Lumumba monument, where so many hundreds of "enemies" of the rebel regime had already been slaughtered, they nearly gave up hope.

Thousands of screaming people jammed the square. Simbas beat at the jeeps with their sticks and rocked them, so that the prisoners thought they would be overturned. Don Parkes was struck in the eye by a stick. Others were burned by lighted cigarettes. From all sides thundered the wild cry, *"Mateke!"*—"Dead Flesh!"

The Americans were pulled from the jeeps in front of the monument. At this critical point General Olenga appeared and ordered them back into the jeeps. Somehow the vehicles made their way through the dense crowd to "President" Gbenye's palace. There Gbenye also appeared and launched into a vindictive speech. Every reference to American "cruelties" brought an ugly responsive roar from the crowd. Gbenye said that Dr. Carlson had been tried for his crimes (in reality, he had never been brought before any tribunal) and would be executed. The crowd screamed for the victims, erupting into that frenzied charade that had become so familiar to the prisoners—going through the grisly motions of striking down imaginary victims, hacking off parts of their bodies and stuffing them into their mouths. *"Mateke!"*

It was at this point that Gbenye announced that Dr. Carlson's execution would be postponed until certain negotiations had been concluded with Kenyatta. The Americans were driven back to prison. Later, *Life* magazine published a dramatic photograph of the prisoners standing before Gbenye. There was Michael, heavily bearded, standing resigned and patient, with Dr. Carlson, two other Consulate men and young Jon Snyder, as Gbenye ranted and the crowd cried for blood. Reports of the demonstrations were carried in the international press on the same day, strongly pointing to the possibility it was all a staged play.

The next day Michael was driven once more to Gbenye's palace. There the rebel "president" showed Michael a message that he wanted him to send, over Michael's name, to the American Embassy in Leopoldville. Michael was ordered to translate the French version into English. A rebel functionary, who apparently had some knowledge of both languages, stood at Michael's shoulder to make certain the sense of the message was not changed. Outside the window Simba guards jeered at Michael. When he had finished translating the massage, it was sent to Leopoldville. It read, in part:

CONFIRM PAUL CARLSON CAPTURED AND CONDEMNED TO DEATH STOP ALL AMERICAN CITIZENS ARE IN DANGER STOP ANY ARRANGEMENT OTHER THAN NEGOTIATION WITH REVOLUTIONARY GOVERNMENT CAN ONLY CAUSE ELIMINATION OF AMERICAN CITIZENS GATHERED IN SEVERAL REGIONS OTHER THAN STAN STOP WITNESSED POPULATION OF ESTIMATED TEN THOUSAND GATHERED IN DEMONSTRATION CONFIRM INSISTENTLY EXECUTION PAUL CARLSON AND EVEN ALL AMERICAN CITIZENS STOP REVOLUTIONARY GOVERNMENT AUTHORITIES SINCERELY DESIRE INITIATE NEGOTIATIONS BEFORE IT TOO LATE STOP DURING NEGOTIATIONS MUST PROHIBIT USE BY TSHOMBE OF US AID FURNISHED HIM TO ATTACK REGIONS CONTROLLED BY REVOLUTIONARY GOVERNMENT STOP ASK YOU PARTICULARLY INTERVENE EFFECTIVELY WITH TSHOMBE OBTAIN CEASE FIRE DURING THESE NEGOTIATIONS OR RISK COMPROMISE DESIRED RESULTS STOP CONFIRM WITH CERTAINTY THAT ONLY WAY SAVE CARLSON AND OTHER AMERICAN SUBJECTS STOP IN NAME ALL AMERICAN CITIZENS IN POPULAR CONGOLESE REPUBLIC AND FOR PRESTIGE OF USA REQUEST INITIATION NEGOTIATIONS WHICH CONSTITUTE OUR LAST CHANCE STOP IN CASE OF DELAY I SAY FOR MYSELF AND FOR MY COMPATRIOTS GOODBYE FULL STOP

HOYT
AMCONSUL
STANLEYVILLE

Obviously, the rebels had given up hope of stemming the central government's attack. The most critical stage of the affair had been reached. Revengeful and despairing, the rebels might make their last gesture a dreadful blood bath. I was frantic. "Send in the Marines," I pleaded with Walker Diamante over the phone. "Do *something!*"

Real news was harder than ever to find. Yet by reading between the lines of tiny press dispatches and thinking over hints dropped here and there by Walker, I knew that something *was* being done. Wayne Fredericks flew from Washington to Nairobi, Kenya, and met with East African leaders. It was said that a Red Cross plane might be allowed to evacuate refugees from Stanleyville. Then we read in the paper that Belgian Foreign Minister Paul Henri Spaak had arrived in Washington and talked to Governor Harriman and other United States officials, the talks supposedly having to do with NATO. Branson and I guessed that it was, rather, the Congo that Spaak had come to discuss.

A rebel spokesman finally appeared in Nairobi; it was apparent that he did not want to discuss the release of hostages. He wanted unconditional assurances that the drive on Stanleyville would be halted. The central government forces were drawing closer, but they still had many miles to travel and rebel patience might give way at any moment. Then we heard an electrifying report on our radio in Arizona. Belgian paratroopers had been flown by American planes to Ascension Island, off the west coast of Africa. The tension became a torture. I no longer slept at night. Charlotte moved in with me.

It was November 23. I didn't dare leave the house, for I knew that there would soon be important news. One radio report threw me into even deeper depression: the rebels had removed all prisoners from Stanleyville. At about midnight I had a call from Washington. It was Walker Diamante.

"The paratroopers have gone in, Jo, but we have no news yet of Michael and his staff."

"But it said on the radio they've taken the prisoners away," I said.

"I don't think that's right," Walker said. "We have every reason to believe they've never been taken out of town."

I sat by the phone. In my mind's eye I could see the Belgian paratroopers dropping into the city. What would the rebels' reaction be? At this point I turned off my imagination.

The phone rang again. It was Walker. The first reports out of Stanleyville said that the operation had been a success, but that some of the hostages had been hurt. Nothing more. I hung up and waited. Now the reports were flooding in over the radio. Belgian paratroopers had captured the airport and were fighting their way into the city. They had counted the bodies of nine slain hostages. It was now two A.M., Tucson time.

Fifteen minutes later the phone rang again. It was Walker's voice: "Jo, he's out. He's on his way to Leopoldville." Then he broke down in sobs, and Ambassador Joe Palmer took the phone to give me the details.

21 ⋆

On the Flip of a Coin

It had been early morning in Stanleyville. Michael and the others had been taken several days before from the central prison and herded into trucks that were to carry them behind rebel lines in the countryside. But the trucks had broken down. The prisoners had been taken back to Stanleyville and lodged in the Victoria Hotel with a large number of Belgian hostages. Now, just after dawn had broken at six o'clock, the prisoners heard the sound of planes overhead. Somebody yelled that he saw parachutes. There was great excitement in the hotel, but no one knew exactly what was happening.

Forty-five minutes later a band of Simbas appeared and ordered all the hostages out into the street. There were about 250 men, women and children. Colonel Opepe drove up and told the prisoners they were to be marched to the airport to prevent its bombardment by

American and Belgian planes. The prisoners detected the sound of small-arms fire in the distance.

The Simbas, some of them armed with automatic weapons, ordered the prisoners to move ahead. The sound of shooting drew closer. The Americans were scattered throughout the length of the line, Michael and Dave Grinwis up front, but Dr. Carlson and others well in the rear. Near the Congo Palace Hotel the column was ordered to turn right toward the main road that led to the airport. Suddenly a truck roared around the corner, carrying a group of Simbas, who shouted at Opepe, "They're already at the airport!"

Opepe ordered the column to halt and made all the prisoners sit down in the street. There was a great deal of confusion among the Simbas. The staccato of small-arms fire drew closer. The Simbas appeared to be frightened rather than angry.

No one knew what touched off the slaughter. Michael said afterward that he saw one of the young Simbas, standing within ten feet of him, swing his rifle slightly upward and then almost casually open fire on the seated hostages. Another Simba fired into the crowd with an automatic weapon. Panic spread among the prisoners. Some fell dead in the first volley. Others jumped to their feet and began running for cover. Ernie Houle threw himself flat on the ground and pretended to be dead. Phyllis Rine, the young missionary who had cared for Evans just a few months before, was cut down by rifle fire and died instantly. Dr. Paul Carlson ran for a brick wall nearby. As he tried to get over it he was shot dead. Michael moved when the others did. He fell, got up and ran on, with bullets hitting all around him. He dashed into an alley and crawled behind a wall. There was the sound of shooting, of people running and shouting.

Then the firing stopped as abruptly as it had begun. Michael remained behind the wall for a few more minutes. Looking down the street, he saw a woman appear on a nearby balcony, a baby in her arms. She looked cautiously up and down the street, but did not go back inside the house. Michael came out from behind the wall, and there, walking toward him, carrying a submachine gun, was a Belgian paratrooper.

While I cried for happiness into a phone in Arizona, Michael and the other surviving Americans were aboard a plane bound for Leopoldville. They had been ordered to leave Stanleyville immediately. The Belgian paratroopers remained behind to search for other hostages and gather the bodies of the thirty-two Americans and Europeans slain in that brief but dreadful volley. In the days and weeks that followed, hundreds of other innocent hostages were brutally murdered in other parts of the Congo, while many more were saved. My joy was tempered by the thought that other families had spent weeks of agonized waiting only to have their loved ones cut down just at the moment of release.

There was tremendous excitement around our house now. The children were all out of bed, chattering and laughing. As I had promised to do, I called the Tucson paper to give them the news of Michael's rescue, and they sent a photographer to the house to get pictures of me and the children. Messages of congratulations began to pour in. There was a call from Dean Rusk in Washington.

"Thank you for being so patient, Mrs. Hoyt," the Secretary said. "I wanted you to know how thankful we all are that your husband is safe."

Best of all (a miracle!) was Michael's voice. The phone call had been arranged by the State Department with the assistance of the Air Force. From Leopoldville the call was relayed to an American Air Force base in Germany, and then on to a base in Arizona and into our home. It was a "patch call," where only one party can speak at a time. Our conversation was breathless and absurd.

"I love you, Michael. Over."

"I love you, Jo. Over."

"How are you? Over."

"Fine. How are the kids? Over."

And then, when the call had been completed, there was the voice of an operator in Germany, signing off. "Oh, ma'am," she said with great feeling, "I'm *so* happy for you!"

Sleep, now that relief had come, was still not possible. Other newspapers were calling, and so were friends. The State Department called again. Had Mi-

chael said when he was coming home? Now I was
passing along information to the Department. Yes, he
would fly to New York on Thursday. They also asked
me to find out, if Michael called again, whether the
four other Consulate men would arrive with him (Michael being the only married man among them and so
the most likely to call a second time). It was only when
I had hung up that I was aware of the exact day on
which Michael would return. Thursday, which had
held no meaning for me until that moment was, I suddenly realized, Thanksgiving!

In Leopoldville, where he had arrived wearing torn
pants, a tattered shirt and scuffed shoes, Michael borrowed what clothes he could. Bob Blake, the deputy
chief of Mission, lent him a suit, and Ambassador
Mac Godley gave him his overcoat for the trip home.
The next day I caught a glimpse of Michael on television, answering a reporter's question. Since the clothes
he wore did not appear to fit him properly, I rushed to a
men's store and bought new clothes for his return.

Waiting for Michael in Leopoldville when he arrived
was a cable from the Secretary of State:

ACTION AMEMBASSY LEOPOLDVILLE
PLEASE PASS TO HOYT FROM THE SECRETARY
THE ENTIRE DEPARTMENT JOINS ME IN EXPRESSING TO
YOU AND YOUR STAFF OUR GRATITUDE AND RELIEF AT YOUR
LIBERATION AFTER THREE HARROWING MONTHS STOP DUR-
ING THAT TIME YOUR WELFARE AND SAFETY HAVE BEEN
UPPERMOST IN OUR MINDS STOP IN SPITE OF THE HUMILIA-
TIONS YOU HAVE SUFFERED AND THE DIFFICULT CONDITIONS

UNDER WHICH YOU HAVE LIVED YOU HAVE ALL DISCHARGED
YOUR DUTIES IN THE HIGHEST TRADITIONS OF THE FOREIGN
SERVICE AND WE EXTEND OUR SINCEREST CONGRATULATIONS
ON YOUR FORTITUDE AND COURAGE STOP WE ALL LOOK FOR-
WARD TO HAVING YOU BACK WITH US AGAIN STOP PLEASE
EXTEND TO MESSRS GRINWIS HOULE STAUFFER AND PARKES
MY SIMILAR ADMIRATION FOR THEIR DEVOTION TO THEIR
DUTY

RUSK

In Tucson, I was just as frantically making arrangements to fly to New York. The State Department had invited me to meet Michael when he arrived from Leopoldville at John F. Kennedy Airport. Wednesday night
I was on my way.

Thanksgiving Day, November 26, was chilly and gray
in New York, but even in our tropical posts I never remember a day that seemed to me so bright. I arrived at
Kennedy Airport early. I found Jim O'Sullivan and Dr.
Lewis K. Woodward, director of the Department's Medical Division, already on hand. They had flown up from
Washington on the Air Force plane that was to take all
of us back there later in the day. We learned that Michael's plane from Leopoldville would be forty-five minutes late. After 110 days of a different kind of waiting,
these last moments seemed almost too much to ask of
me.

A large crowd was assembled at the airport, many of
them representing newspapers and television networks.
Wooden barriers were erected to keep the crowd in
hand, and the health authorities were warning every-

one to keep away from the plane when it landed. Finally the big plane was down, rolling across the field toward us and pulling up in front of the terminal. The door swung open and a figure appeared in the doorway and—it was Michael! Guards and officials pressed around him as he came down the steps. He seemed to be confused by the commotion around him, his head turning this way and that as people threw questions at him. Then his glance turned in my direction and he saw me. In a moment he was running through the crowd, pushing people away, and then I was in his arms.

I was completely overwhelmed. I don't remember whether we said anything to each other, and if so, what it was. The anxiety of many months had melted away. I was content to remain there beside Michael forever, but slowly we became aware that other people had clustered around us and were trying to say something to us. They were telling us to get aboard the plane for Washington.

I couldn't take my eyes off Michael. He was thinner, having dropped from 195 pounds to 175, and there were dark circles under his eyes. The borrowed suit and overcoat emphasized these superficial changes. But as we walked together toward the other plane, I saw that he was in excellent spirits. The ordeal had not damaged him, either psychologically or physically. The Simbas had not broken him.

There was a great deal of confusion about whether

Michael should be asked to speak to the reporters, now straining behind the barriers. It was *yes*, then *no*, finally *yes*. At last he was led away to answer a few questions. He told the press that he was feeling fine but regretted that Dr. Carlson and the others were not able to escape. After answering only a few questions, he was pulled away by the officials and we boarded the plane. The rest of the Consulate staff and their families joined us aboard. En route to Washington, Michael and the others were examined by Dr. Woodward and pronounced fit.

"They're okay now," the State Department physician said. "The reunion with their families was the best tonic they could have had."

The climax of the Washington trip was to be a reception given by Dean Rusk at the State Department. But first Michael wanted to make himself presentable. Though I thought he looked just fine the way he was, he said he would feel better with a decent haircut. Toward the end of the ordeal in Stanleyville, with all sorts of pressures upon them and the possibility that other African leaders might arrive there for negotiations, the rebel leaders decided to tidy up their hostages. All the Americans wore heavy growths of beard, and had not seen a barber since the city's fall. Rebel leaders gave them the choice of having their beards pulled out (an old local custom, apparently) or cut off.

Michael and the others preferred to trust their luck with the barber assigned to them. This fellow happened to be an itinerant Greek who had married a Congolese woman and settled on the outskirts of Stanleyville. He clipped the hostages' beards and hair but his workmanship left something to be desired. Now, when Michael sat down in the barber's chair in Washington, the barber looked him over and clucked his tongue.

"Where in the hell did you get *this* haircut?" he asked.

Michael simply shrugged. He felt that the story was too long to go into.

On Friday we had lunch with Governor Harriman. There were more press conferences. And in the evening there was the reception at the State Department, and Michael learned he was to be given the Secretary's Award, the highest honor in the Foreign Service.

I seemed to be drifting on a cloud of happiness. Here were the most distinguished men in the Department gathered together to honor Michael and the brave men who had suffered with him in Stanleyville. Ahead of us lay a reunion with the children and the drive home from the airport to see the "Welcome Daddy!" signs they had prepared for his arrival. Then there would be a tour of duty at the Operations Center in Washington, and later Michael would serve under Governor Williams in the African Bureau. And finally we hoped for the realization of Michael's wish: his eventual return to duty in Africa.

We had come a long way since that afternoon in Chicago eight years before when Michael had bounded up the steps of the Field Museum to tell me that he had passed his examination for the Foreign Service. Our hopes had been fulfilled. We had learned much, and grown much as human beings, through our contacts with people all over the world. Our children had grown to awareness in a variety of lands, which, we like to think, is an incomparable preparation for the day when they will be able to lead their own lives as mature American citizens. In gaining these advantages, Michael had not only been able to serve his country, but in the words of the Secretary's Award, to serve it with "outstanding courage and dignity in the highest traditions of the Foreign Service."

He had not earned that award easily. This was brought home to us at the reception when Dean Rusk walked over to congratulate Michael. I took the opportunity to thank the Secretary for his long struggle to have Michael brought home to me. The Secretary smiled, took a half dollar from the pocket of his jacket and flipped it in the air.

"Tell me, Mrs. Hoyt," he asked. "At one point I wasn't worth the flip of a coin in all this business, was I?"

It was a sobering thought. The power and prestige of the Secretary of State, backed by the greatest nation in the world, were not sufficient for 110 days to offset the flip of a coin by an unstable rebel commander, one extra sip of beer by a tipsy Simba, one added minute to the dash of a Belgian paratrooper as he came around a corner to cut short a pointless massacre. The slightest pressure to the scales might have frustrated all the Department's efforts, and Michael would not have been standing beside me at that moment.

The reception was over. It was to this increasingly complicated world that Michael, the rest of us following, would return to take up his work in the Foreign Service.